KU-764-272

A
Solemn
Joy

ELAINE BROWN

KINGSWAY PUBLICATIONS
EASTBOURNE

Copyright © Elaine Brown 1986

First published 1986

All rights reserved.
No part of this publication may be reproduced or
transmitted in any form or by any means, electronic
or mechanical, including photocopy, recording, or any
information storage and retrieval system, without
permission in writing from the publisher.

ISBN 0 86065 354 4

Unless otherwise indicated biblical quotations are from the
Revised Standard Version, copyrighted 1946, 1952,
© 1971, 1973 by the Division of Christian Education of the
National Council of the Churches of
Christ in the USA

GNB = Good News Bible
© American Bible Society 1976

Front cover photo: Hans Reinhard, Bruce Coleman Ltd

Printed in Great Britain for
KINGSWAY PUBLICATIONS LTD
Lottbridge Drove, Eastbourne, E. Sussex BN23 6NT by
Cox & Wyman Ltd, Reading.
Typeset by CST, Eastbourne.

PHIL & GRACE SIMPSON
3 GALLOWDEN AVENUE
ARBROATH
DD11 3EX
0241 74691

A SOLEMN JOY

For all who will recognize
themselves in these pages,
and to whom I owe so much.

Contents

	Author's Note	10
	Introduction	11
1.	The Answer at Last?	15
2.	Pain and Joy	33
3.	Sting in the Tail	44
4.	*Is* God Good?	59
5.	'There *Is* a Way through This!'	71
6.	A New Seeing	97
7.	The Crisis of Acceptance	123
8.	'He Kens It A'!'	138
9.	'Love Me for Myself Alone . . .'	158
10.	The Inescapable Mosaic	170
11.	Nothing Can Win against God!	177
	Conclusion	187

God, Thou art Love! I build my faith on that!

I know Thee, Thou hast kept my path and made
Light for me in the darkness—tempering sorrow,
So that it reached me like a solemn joy:
It were too strange that I should doubt Thy love.

Robert Browning

Author's Note

Much of the material used in this book has come from a detailed diary. This was written mainly because it offered frequent personal release during difficult circumstances. This book is an attempt to go beyond that and share the ground of all hope for all those who are suffering now, or have been through a difficult time, or perhaps know of others who are going through their own 'time of trial' and wish to understand better some of the hopes and fears they may be experiencing.

Most names have been changed, and some facts have been omitted or slightly altered in order to protect the identities of those who, in so many ways, have contributed to this story.

Introduction

It was eleven o'clock on a warm midsummer's evening. Blinds had been drawn across the wide windows, plunging our small hospital ward into shadowy gloom. Everything was quiet. Even the dimly-lit corridor seemed empty. Silence, except for the steady, even breathing of my two room-mates who were already fast asleep. Despite weariness, I was wide awake. The same sinister fear kept tugging at my mind, threatening the frail calm I was beginning to discover through clinging tightly to Jesus. I must somehow escape this renewed onslaught of fear, perhaps by turning my mind in a completely different direction?

I remembered the stereo headphones a visitor had left the previous day, together with a wide selection of cassette music—symphonies, concertos, oratorios. Days and weeks of listening! A recording of Vivaldi's evocative 'Four Seasons' lay on top of the pile and so, in the semi-darkness, I fitted it into the player, put on the headphones, and lay back.

Suddenly the magnificent music burst out, echoing round the huge concert hall in which it was being played, lifting me far away from the small silent hospital ward. I closed my eyes, imagining myself to be there in the audience, beneath the tall graceful pillars and ornate vaulted ceilings which so perfectly match Vivaldi's music. What grandeur! What a welcome contrast to the sterile white of that confining room. I began to relax, tempor-

11

arily forgetting my fear and revelling in the delight of such exquisite music . . . And it was then, amid this unexpected joy, that Jesus set a new idea in my mind. 'Write down what has happened. Find relief by putting it all into words, words which could one day offer you a bond with others.'

Several months have passed since that June evening and now, looking back, I want to try to share the experiences which led up to those moments of 'new seeing', as well as what has happened since. It is hard to do so, and for this reason I feel somewhat hesitant. On the one hand I long to walk away and forget the sadness and fear, yet on the other I sense a need to stop first and search for something of lasting value to take on with me into the future. Only then can adversity begin to hold meaning and become unexpectedly creative, drawing me closer to God and so to others, in a new bond of understanding.

At one time I was no more than an observer standing on the outside of suffering, looking in. But it is all different now.

*   *   *

Let me start by explaining that we live in an attractive Aberdeenshire village. Our wooden house, one of several built by the Council to accommodate oil-related personnel, is situated alongside the River Don. From the back windows we can look out over woods and fields on the river's further bank, which stretch away to a distant ridge of hills, collectively known as Bennachie. We arrived seven years ago, soon after my Scots husband, Les, obtained work as an airline pilot involved with North Sea oil operations. Since then our three youngsters have made Scotland their home and we have been glad for them to spend so much of their childhood in this beautiful northern corner.

The events shared in this book began in early January when our nineteen-year-old daughter, Rachel, had just moved to nearby Aberdeen for radiography training at the Infirmary, and our fifteen-year-old twins, Stuart and Murray, were working towards O-grade examinations, Murray being a student at the village academy and Stuart at a public day school in the city.

But while the youngsters were busy studying and I was well occupied at home, Les was finding each day very long and empty. He had lost his good flying position almost three years earlier and had since passed through a distressing period of unemployment.* All enquiries about flying work in Britain and abroad had drawn a blank, leaving us more bewildered than ever. Sometimes Les was able to pick up short-term labouring work sorting potatoes, cleaning machinery, and cutting steel cables. He also spent six months giving temporary flying assistance to a small mission group in Florida, USA. It was soon after this trip that, to our delight, Les was offered a captain's position with a British airline. It seemed that our long-awaited answer had come at last! Then, on the very day he was due to start, Les discovered that his vital aircrew medical certificate was about to be withdrawn. X-rays taken a few weeks earlier had revealed a degenerative neck condition which, though causing only occasional dizziness, could not be cured. It meant Les would have permanently to forfeit his commercial pilot's licence. He would not be able to fly again.

We were very shaken by this news. It was October and a long, bleak northern winter was beginning. I remember the sense of foreboding as the last golden leaves drifted down from our riverside beeches and floated away towards the open sea. Soon the woods would be empty and still, the tall reeds at the water's edge would shrivel and die, and the birds (even our tuneful robin) would fall silent in the biting cold. The heavy sadness of circumstances seemed more irksome than ever before. Which direction should we take now? What was God trying to say to us in this new bewildering context? Had we become insensitive and blind?

* Described in my earlier book *Grounded*, The Diary of an Unemployment (Lion Publishing 1979).

We were tired of asking questions, tired of searching for answers. Tired of trying and trying to find work. 'Lord, please give us a breakthrough soon. Les can't keep going much longer,' I prayed as November dragged past and the long winter darkness closed in on our northern world.

Then, in mid-December, a friend handed us a news-paper cutting which advertised the need for an assistant warden at a large Christian conference centre elsewhere in Scotland. Les was immediately interested and phoned for an application form which he filled in and posted back by return.

We celebrated that Christmas and New Year's Eve with fresh hopefulness. The old year was ending at last.

'We'll never have to live through all those hard experiences again. They're over and gone!' we reminded ourselves, and the thought triggered a whole new upsurge of hope.

I

The Answer at Last?

A sunlit dawn woke us on New Year's Day and soon afterwards a dozen wild whooper swans flew directly overhead, their huge wings rhythmically sawing through the still morning air. What an impressive fly past with which to celebrate so special a day! Later, when washing up the breakfast dishes, Les caught sight of a squirrel leaping from branch to branch of the riverside beeches with astonishing agility, not showing the slightest sign of winter sleepiness. Perhaps he was delighting in the mild, gleaming morning too.

One suppertime a few days later Stuart turned to Les and said, 'Dad, you *will* have work soon. I know it!'

His words expressed my own growing confidence.

'Yes, I'm sure of it too,' I added.

Les hesitated, smiling a little. 'Maybe. We'll see!'

My confidence was further boosted the following week when we were both invited to visit the conference centre prior to Les's proposed interview for the assistant warden's post. He and four others had been short-listed from the numerous applicants and we were beginning to get really excited.

'God must have allowed Les's flying career to come to an end so he could lead you in a completely different direction, and maybe this new opportunity is exactly what he has had in mind all along!' friends encouraged us. Their words kept going through my mind that January afternoon as we were shown over the large, im-

pressive centre with its wide views across a river gorge to
steep snow-covered slopes beyond. It was all so beautiful!
A place where I knew Les would rediscover the pleasure
of being needed and the satisfaction of making his own
particular contribution.

Once Les's interview was over we found it difficult to
wait for the result. Day after day went by and still no
letter came. I tried to reassure myself by remembering
that God could foresee all that was going to happen. He
had it all under control.

'Don't you find that a comfort?' I said to Les over our
soup and sandwich lunch one day, but he only frowned.

'No, not really.'

I was disappointed and a little hurt because he hadn't
appreciated my eagerly-shared realization, but it continued to be important to me, and the more so now that we
seemed to be right on the brink of a breakthrough. I
could hardly wait for further news.

It came at last. Les and one other applicant were now
neck-and-neck for the post, the other three men having
been eliminated. The following week a second interview
took place, but afterwards the outcome remained inde-
cisive.

'You are both ideally suited to the work and we don't
know which to choose,' the committee explained apolo-
getically. 'May we ask you to wait a few more days and
meanwhile to pray with us concerning a decision?'

What suspense! And how hard it was to be patient,
harder than ever before. Yet we were glad the final decision was being made so carefully and, though I didn't
tell Les, I was all but certain he would be chosen. The
work exactly matched his skills and interests and, besides,
the whole possibility had had a good 'feel' about it right
from the start.

January was creeping past. Before the month ended I
caught sight of a first shy snowdrop trembling in the
fierce wind, and that same morning thought I heard the
excited greeting of a returning oyster-catcher. But no, it
was only a mischievous starling sitting on our rooftop
and mimicking those sleek black and white coastal birds

whose jubilant arrival always announces the start of spring. I was annoyed by the starling's cheek, and the more so when it began to survey nesting prospects under the roof tiles surrounding the outlet of our ventilator pipe!

Despite continuing suspense, life kept to much the same pattern at home with Les spending long hours studying book-keeping (such details would be an asset at the Centre), while I worked on a book which seemed to become more and more exacting as the days went by. When the January snow cleared I began cycling to and from the village shops once more, appreciating the view across to Bennachie on my way home, particularly on sunlit mornings when the nearer peak of Mither Tap stood bold against the sky. It would always be there, reassuringly the same amid the many temporary uncertainties with which we were living.

On one such shopping morning I noticed a neighbour, Annette, pegging out washing, and remembered she would be undergoing a major operation later in the week. I felt for her and the family, and realized how blessed we had all been with good health. Les's dizziness had cleared up now he was on medication, and none of us had so much as suffered from a cold during the damp wintry weather. Despite the long, irksome drag of unemployment we still had the physical strength and stamina with which to face our circumstances. An important asset. That morning, after a bracing cycle ride back from the village, I felt particularly grateful for so rich a blessing.

This awareness of personal good health further contributed to my problem with the book I was writing. Several months before, I had agreed to write in as simple a way as possible on the subject of death, but it was proving to be a very difficult task despite a helpful agent's encouragement. At his suggestion I had talked with people facing a life-threatening illness or the trauma of bereavement, and the more I thought about their words the more I longed to be able to understand, to feel with those encountering so solemn and disturbing a reality.

Yet I could not do so. For all my longing, it was impossible
adequately to project myself into their circumstances.
Would this ultimately cause the book to be of limited use
and relevance? Would it ever be worth publishing? The
nearer I came to completion of the project the more my
doubts grew. Yet I knew I must go on, if only for the
sake of those who, at cost, had shared painful personal
experiences in order to reach out to others. I knew their
stories would make an impact even though my own
understanding was so limited.

*   *   *

One snowy February morning when I was at the upstairs
desk, struggling with the last chapter of the book, we
received the final answer on the assistant warden's post.
In the absence of a letter that morning Les had decided
to phone around 10 a.m. Soon afterwards I heard his
footsteps on the stairs and, in my happy excitement,
hardly dared to look round as he came into the room.
He stopped beside me and touched my shoulder lightly
with his hand.

'I've lost it.'

I didn't move, but sat very still looking out of the
window, seeing a flurry of snowflakes vanish in the river's
cold grey water.

They must have made a mistake. Les was so right for
the post. Didn't they realize this? Didn't they appreciate
his practical abilities, his eager self-giving nature? And
besides, hadn't I felt so sure this was God's wise purpose
for us? Everything about the position was right for Les.
It would be such a worthwhile ministry too, not just any
old job . . .

I couldn't bear to look round and meet Les's eyes, yet
at the same time longed to surround him and somehow
bear the full force of this blow. The deep pain must
inevitably be his, yet perhaps I could, in some measure,
enter into it with him. I stood up and we lingered together by the window for a while, lost in our separate
thoughts. If only they had chosen Les. If only it could

have been a 'yes' at last, instead of yet another 'no'. Had I been misunderstanding God's ordering of events lately, presuming on his plan when all along, from my limited human viewpoint, I could not possibly know it with certainty? But then, why did God allow developments to be clear enough to trigger legitimate confidence, only to thrust us later into sudden confusion and despair? The very strength of my previous confidence now served to accentuate the despair. My mind became too troubled to try and find answers for the 'whys'. I didn't even want answers. I only wanted to persist with questions. How could all our eager hopes have come so suddenly to a complete end? It seemed impossible. Inexplicable.

That evening, after tussling with my tangled thoughts all day I came, slowly and unwillingly, to accept that the 'no' was not a mistake but rather the committee's considered decision after prayer. I began to recognize it as the closing of a door, the shutting away of all that had seemed so full of glad promise. It was not to be ours after all. Then too, for all my quick confidence over previous weeks, I sensed the need to be more guarded in future, not presuming on God and rushing ahead to predict his decisions. I realized that instead of putting confidence in the expected outcome of favourable circumstances, I needed to place it simply in God himself, being glad that he, from an ideal position of complete knowledge, would always have the eventual 'yes' or 'no'. The more I considered this the more I knew it to be an important, basic lesson, yet so difficult to accept in the pain of acute disappointment.

Les and I spent the evening quietly together, saying little, just drawing on the comfort of companionship. I put Les's favourite records on the player, Rachmaninov's 'Rhapsody on a theme of Paganini', Grieg's piano concerto. Such poignant, exquisite music!

Later, when clearing away our cocoa mugs, I came across Les's book-keeping notes on top of the coffee table. He had spent so many long hours eagerly gathering and recording information, and now the sight of all those carefully written pages suddenly compounded the hurt I felt for him. Mingled with this pain was the sharp sadness of having to put aside all thought of involvement at the Centre after living excitedly with the possibility for over a month.

I hardly knew what to say to Les in the long days which followed, for any easy reassurance—'There's sure to be something else!' or 'We won't have to wait much longer!'—was no more than a hollow mockery. Instead I tried to show my concern for Les in a touch, a glance, or by doing something special for him. Even a simple thing like the giant-sized Knickerbocker Glory I concocted for his pudding one lunchtime. I couldn't face a dessert myself, having lost any appetite for fancy food. After our meal that day an occasional but wretched stomach pain suddenly surged back. It took over completely, rendering me incapable of doing anything at all except suffer it out. Within an hour I'd almost mastered it, but Les was concerned.

'You need some advice,' he insisted and, before I could protest that the problem was only due to stress, he telephoned for a doctor's appointment the following morning.

Our Bible reading late that evening was a brief but relevant psalm. One of its phrases lingered in my mind as we went up to bed: 'His faithfulness is everlasting' (Ps 117).

Had I doubted God's faithfulness over all the long months, or through this present bewildering disappointment? No, deep in my heart, I had not doubted. For all the indignant 'whys', the inner certainty remained intact. There *was* going to be eventual good in all that had happened. How, I didn't know, nor when, nor exactly what. I knew only that the Lord's purpose was ultimately to enrich through adversity, and that such an enrichment would far outweigh even the most extreme frustration and despair. It was an idealistic certainty but surely not therefore unreasonable? Didn't all of Christianity point towards a most wonderful and ultimately attainable ideal? Late that night, as I lay awake thinking, I knew I must cling more tightly to this certainty of God's unaltering faithfulness, not letting it slip my grasp. For it was true, despite the puzzle of adverse circumstances; no one had ever proved God to be unfaithful, nor would they do so. People only thought they had after attempting to measure him up against their own mistaken human standards.

Next morning I saw the doctor, who suspected the pain might be caused by gallstones and suggested diagnostic X-rays. It would take about a fortnight for the appointment (in Rachel's department of the hospital) to come through. 'That will give time for the symptoms to clear,' I decided. 'And maybe they'll prove to be of no consequence at all.'

On the way out of the surgery I noticed my neighbour, Annette, sitting in the car while her husband shopped for groceries. She looked quite well and was certainly as bright as ever.

'The operation went fine!' she told me. 'But they're not sure about the future. The problem could start again.' I was amazed at Annette's genuine cheerfulness even after a difficult operation which hadn't, as expected, completely solved her troubles.

*   *   *

Mid-February brought several fierce blizzards, followed by calm sunlit days when our white northern world glistened and gleamed with brief and intense beauty. One afternoon we couldn't resist driving out along a narrow country road, locally called 'The Lord's Throat', which followed the Don upstream. Parking at a forestry centre, we smiled to see each picnic table and bench upholstered with thick pure-white snow cloths and cushions, while all the nearby birches were hung with shining ice beads. 'Let's walk up through the forest!' I suggested to Les. So we took a steep woodland path, enjoying the muffled silence, broken only by the chatter of a few tits high in the pine trees. At one point, where the path opened out onto a forestry road, we came across a ski track and footprints of rabbits, and a dog or fox. The woodland stillness was wonderfully refreshing.

'It's like a whole new world up here!' I told Les, and he nodded.

'But you wouldn't want the snow to linger on for ever, would you?'

When driving home we came across fourteen whooper swans, including two juveniles, foraging in a roadside field of winter grain shoots. It was a thrill to stop and observe those large birds at such close quarters, though the farmer would have been horrified by the trampling of their huge feet. Twilight had crept in when we reached the village, and a veil of smoke from hearth fires was pink-tinged in the pale glow of sunset.

'Not long until spring!' I reminded Les and he smiled a little, his mind preoccupied. I knew that he was now forcing himself to draw up a whole new plan of action in his search for employment. Where should he try next? Which leads should he follow? Who would be interested in a man of his age with few relevant paper qualifications and almost no experience other than in aviation?

Towards the end of the month I received word from the doctor about the X-ray results. His diagnosis had been proved correct. 'So I'm afraid your gall bladder will have to be removed.'

It came as quite a shock. I hadn't thought the problem was severe enough to require surgery, so instead of simply accepting the fact, I tried to dismiss it by keeping particularly busy around the house during those first few days. Les was working on an interesting idea too, and I deliberately focused my attention on this new possibility. He had contacted the mission group with which we'd once worked abroad, offering help in an administrative capacity. The mission leaders were immediately interested and suggested a visit to their home base in England.

Les's trip south went well and we began seriously to consider the mission's proposals, though we were cautious about a move at so critical a time in our boys' education. Les was keeping in touch with local work possibilities too, and one such was the need for monitors in a new gas-flow control room at one of the city's large oil complexes. People with experience in reading information from dials were particularly encouraged to apply. Who better than a pilot! But, after contacting the company concerned, Les was pessimistic about his chances.

'They'll be swamped with applicants because they've advertised so widely,' he told me and I noted the hopelessness in his voice. He often spoke like that now. I knew, too, that he was very tired. He had taken temporary work as a porter and although glad of this opportunity to provide for family needs rather than accept unemployment benefit, he found each day very hard and long.

We were both caught up in our own different inner struggles while at the same time trying to reach out in understanding and support to one another. Though he said little, I knew Les was feeling for me in my anxiety about the approaching operation, yet I hated for him to have this additional concern when he himself was facing so much. Anxious to spare him, I determined to keep my own fear to myself.

I was beginning to wake early each morning, and in the long pre-dawn darkness exaggerated dread of the operation filled my mind. It was always my first thought and almost impossible to shake off. I am myself a trained nurse, so why should I be so full of apprehension? Was it because I knew too much, and also because the thought of being a patient went greatly against the grain? My mind began to visualize every detail of what would lie ahead: admission to the ward, physical examinations, preparations for surgery, the actual cholecystectomy operation. I couldn't help remembering nursing days spent 'running' for surgeons in the theatre, and how we had often been called to watch the first incision and subsequent procedures. I found myself going on to imagine what waking up afterwards would be like; the pain, the drip, the embarrassing total dependence upon others. My mind stopped there. It wouldn't go further. I didn't think much about recovery or the joy of returning home. The dread side of it all was too prominent.

Hating the whole idea of the operation, I resented its

intrusion and spoiling of the healthy image of which I'd
been so proud. Why did this have to happen just when I
needed to be well and strong in order to support and
encourage Les? It was another of those tiresome 'whys'
to which there could be no adequate answer. The only
way to cope effectively with the problem was quietly to
accept and go through with its implications. But I was in
no mind for meek acquiescence, prizing independence
too much. Nor did I want my predictable daily routine
disturbed. As an ordered, disciplined person, routine
had become extremely important to me, a source of
security. 'I'm needed here at home to keep everything
running smoothly,' I decided. 'No other person can
achieve quite the same effect.' I baulked at the thought
of having to hand over temporarily to anyone else, even
Les. Would he think to wash the bathroom floor each
week or wipe the cat's muddy pawmarks off the window-
sills? Would he know to store cakes and biscuits in separate tins, or seal the bread bag tightly with a clothes
peg?

'Such small, silly details!' people would have said if
they'd known what was churning round and round in
my mind. Yes, they *were* small and ridiculous but somehow they'd grown big and insistent. While trying to make
light of the physical problem (which was apparently quite
a serious matter), I had allowed trivialities constantly to
irritate and disturb me.

'Lord, my thinking is in a mess,' I prayed early on one
of those mornings. 'I'm caught right in the middle of it
all. Please help me to step aside and get things in per-
spective, eventually seeing my situation from your angle
instead of mine.'

Stepping aside was difficult. I had to work at it by
deliberately focusing thoughts away from personal circumstances so that I could then be open to outside things,
finding much-needed relief and enjoyment in them. One
such was the hectic cry of a first oyster-catcher at 7 a.m.
on the last Monday of the month. A marvellous sound!
Within days flocks of these noisy birds, black and white
against blue, were bustling back and forth across the sky,

shrieking at all hours of the day and night. Oyster-catchers live constantly in high gear, determined to stir everyone else up too. They're complete extroverts! Later that same morning, when admiring the first bright golden crocus in our side garden, I looked up and saw a row of young starlings along our rooftop. So that explained the muffled chirping and chattering above our upstairs ceilings! The parent birds *had* had the cheek to squeeze in beside our ventilator pipe and set up house. How many more rowdy batches of offspring were they likely to produce before the summer was out?

March began with two or three sparkling spring days, and on the Saturday of that first week Les and I drove across country to Craigievar Castle, noticing budding pussy-willow trees en route and also several snowdrops clustered along the banks of a small bubbling burn. Here and there on higher hill slopes the last traces of snow were spread like scraps of lace across tufts of coarse meadow grass. The well-kept castle stood remote and majestic as ever above the valley. It will always be my favourite, and I enjoyed it all over again as we walked up the beech-lined driveway and stood back to gaze up at those high turrets. How calm and quiet it all was! Only the gentle bleat of nearby ewes and lambs broke the silence.

'We really need to take time off like this in order to get things back in proportion,' I commented to Les. 'Once you can persuade yourself to relax, difficulties recede a little.'

We talked on as we strolled through the castle grounds, up-dating thoughts and plans.

'I think we should leave the possibility of moving south in abeyance for the time being while you get over your operation,' Les said. 'The mission folk will understand. Meanwhile we can see if anything develops on the local scene.'

He paused, considering a further idea. 'In fact, maybe we should set April 30th as a deadline and say that if something permanent materializes up here by then we'll stay, if not we'll interpret the lack of an opening as God's

confirmation that we should move down to join the
mission. What do you think?'

I was more than glad to accept the proposal. Having a
firm plan in mind would help to offset the frustration of
living with uncertainties and would also give us a clearcut goal upon which to focus in prayer and trust. Maybe,
too, Jesus was wanting us to learn the discipline of looking to him just for the 'next steps' rather than for guidance about far-reaching strides. He knew it would ultimately be much easier for us that way.

Dark shadows were lengthening across the wide lawns
as we made our way back to the car, but the far hills were
still golden in the sunlight and, over to the west, a single
cloud lay like a plumed feather against the pale sky. A
sudden thought came to me.

'Isn't it a blessing we aren't moving to the Centre after
all this spring!' I said, squeezing Les's hand. 'It would
have been impossible for you to cope with the demands
over there as well as with trying to run the home while
I'm away.'

'Yes, I've been thinking that, too.'

                    *   *   *

One morning, a short while later, a brown envelope arrived from the hospital giving my admission date—April
20th. Over a month to wait, but somehow the sight of
the card and the 'Information for Patients' booklet which
accompanied it filled me with renewed dread. I sat down
with a cup of coffee and read through the details: how
to get to the hospital, what to bring, visiting hours, ward
routine, etc. It all sounded so simple and straightforward,
almost casual. If only they knew how a patient felt, how
the inner tension increased as soon as an actual date
loomed ahead. I had never even imagined a patient's
apprehension could be so keen and strong.

A few days later Rachel arrived home from the hospital, 'To study for my physics exam and to take care of
you for a little while, Mum!' she explained, her large
dark eyes full of concern because she knew I had had

further attacks of pain. It was thoughtful of her, but in my stubbornness I found it hard to respond gratefully and allow myself to be cared for. Was Jesus intending to release me from such staunch self-sufficiency in the coming weeks? Did I want him to? I was not at all sure, for it would mean relinquishing my valued independence, but then neither did I want to hurt those dear to me. During that week as Rachel tried hard to relieve me of shopping, cooking and cleaning I sensed, with growing concern, that the coming time of inactivity was going to be a test on all fronts.

But then, the inactivity also had its positive side. At the family's insistence (all four of them had taken to nagging me by now), I had begun to rest on the settee each afternoon, using the time for quiet prayer and reading. I started on R. T. Kendall's book *Who By Faith*,* based on the New Testament 'faith chapter' of Hebrews 11, and was immediately impressed by the fact that those people of faith *believed God, full stop*. They didn't first demand clearcut evidence of how God was working, or why. They simply believed, even when circumstances seemed crazy and meaningless from a human viewpoint. Their belief, based entirely on the faithfulness and righteousness of God, was completely independent of circumstances. Because of this they enjoyed total security. They were invulnerable.

As all these thoughts went through my mind I became more and more impressed by such a faith, realizing it to be an essential for everyone, not just a privilege for the chosen few. Then one Sunday, over our early morning tea, Les made a comment which straightaway underlined the fact that 'believing God, full stop' was important in our own circumstances too.

'If only God would *show* me something,' Les said, his face sad. 'If only he'd made our situation clear. Even a *little* more clear. Then I could feel encouraged in faith. But he doesn't. There's nothing. Nothing at all . . ."

As I thought of Les's words, feeling for him in his bewilderment, I began to see that sometimes God in-

* R. T. Kendall *Who By Faith* (Hodder and Stoughton 1981).

tended there to be nothing at all, simply so that we too could learn to believe God, full stop. This was the faith he wanted to nurture in us through the enigma of adversity, the utterly secure faith he waited to give so we could be enriched, and made safe and invulnerable as well. The thought of this intrigued and greatly attracted me, and I found myself reconsidering it many more times in the months which followed.

It was not that God left us without practical evidence of his working in our situation. Clearcut requests were often heard and granted so we might be encouraged by answers to our prayers. One such answer came when Les received word from the oil company. They had shortlisted him for the gas-flow monitoring job and interviews would be taking place within two weeks. What huge excitement!

'Could you buy me a new shirt?' Les asked happily. 'One with a stiff collar, so I'll be presentable.'

I felt so glad for him, and it was certainly interesting that, just when we were considering a move south, the possibility of permanent local work should present itself.

Easter came in the midst of our excitement and on Good Friday Rachel helped me make a large batch of sticky, spicy hot cross buns. Once they had all been baked I took time off quietly to consider Jesus' words from the cross. What a graphic portrayal of his selflessness! I was moved by his detailed concern for those close by—callous soldiers, a distraught thief, a grieving mother, a totally bewildered disciple. As I read on I longed to love and appreciate Jesus the more, for such self-giving had to evoke a matching response. I longed really to know him in that deep transforming oneness which couldn't be expressed in words. The longing was like a growing hunger which would only be satisfied by Jesus' giving of himself more and more fully to me. But I hesitated at that point, not sure if I wanted the radical personal changes involved in such a receiving. And so my hesitancy checked the hunger, inevitably limiting Jesus from giving all he so richly intended for me.

Easter Saturday brought mingled wind and snow

showers, with just a few snatches of sunlight. But on Easter Day the whole world was gleaming beneath a cloudless sky, and as we set out for church we noticed the first wild daffodils in full bloom on the far bank of the river. The communion service was particularly significant to me because that poignant Good Friday scene was still vivid in my mind. For all the exultation of Jesus' resurrection, the suffering somehow refused to be forgotten and I sensed that in some measure it must always be there, an interweaving of ultimate anguish with ultimate love; and then the inexpressible joy!

Suffering kept creeping back into the corners of my mind. I didn't want to become morbidly preoccupied with the subject, yet an accumulation of circumstances (in the wider world as well as within our family) had forced me to consider its reality in greater detail, and to search for some meaning and value to offset all the questioning and sorrow. And that Easter, more than on any before, I began to love and to long for Jesus with a new intensity, simply because I now recognized his complete identification with human wretchedness and suffering. He really did understand. And as the risen Christ, he waited to go on into the future with me, not merely alongside but right inside, choosing to bear my pain even as I must bear it too.

*   *   *

Les's work interview was scheduled for April 18th, a couple of days before my admission to hospital. Eager to leave everything in good order at home, I had made out a 'things to be done' list, and during that last week worked extra hard around the house. One afternoon, feeling weary, I lay down on the settee only to be faced by a sudden fierce return of fear. I tried to fight it off, then thought, how about healing? Could Jesus heal me here and now? Would he? How marvellous that would be! Think of the impression it would make on everyone!

Then I hesitated. The idea thrilled yet also disturbed me. For all my apprehension, I had now accepted the

inevitability of the operation. My mind was settled about
the matter and, in my carefully ordered way, I'd mapped
out a new routine for the next few weeks. A sudden
readjustment was unacceptable, I couldn't face it. Then,
after such a frank admission, I felt ashamed. Not want to
be instantly healed? It seemed incredible. Friends would
have been shocked if they'd known, particularly those
who had promised specific prayer for such a healing.

'Lord, please help me with this,' I found myself asking.
'I'm torn between knowing I ought to ask for instant
healing, yet not wanting to . . .'

I lay there for a long time, gazing out at the silver sky,
seeing black-headed gulls skimming back and forth above
the river. Then very gently, almost imperceptibly at first, I
sensed Jesus' closeness, his suggestion of something quite
different for me to consider.

'I want you to accept, to leave it all with me and believe
in the reality of my goodness to you without needing to
know more. Will you let me take you through each part
of this unwelcome experience? Will you trust in my ability
even to turn it to value for you?'

I began to let go, opening myself to Jesus just a little
more. Yes, ultimately I *did* want him to turn my circumstances to good in whatever way he had planned. Perhaps
part of the purpose would be to take me through several
valuable learning experiences. Hadn't I had an inkling
of this already?

The day for Les's interview came. Everything went
well and the company promised to notify him of the
result within two or three weeks. That would bring us to
the end of April. Just the right timing!

Fifteen men were being considered for five places.
'Which gives me no more than a one-in-three chance!'
Les reminded us over supper the same evening. But the
boys weren't going to be discouraged.

'Don't worry, you'll get it Dad. Just you wait and see!'
they both insisted.

Next day I tackled a mountain of laundry, filled the
cake tins, and made out menus to help Les and the boys
as they fended for themselves.

'Why are you doing so much?' Les kept objecting, but he didn't understand how I needed to pour out my love and caring for them all before leaving the following morning. I wanted the family to come across small extra touches so they'd be assured of my continuing concern, like the large chocolate bars I had bought to slip under their pillows as a bedtime surprise on my first night away.

At last, when every item on the check list had been ticked off, I went upstairs to have a bath and wash my hair. It was early evening and I remembered a friend's phone call earlier in the day.

'Make a point of listening to Radio 4 at seven-thirty tonight,' she'd insisted. 'They'll be interviewing David Watson about his recent cancer operation.'

I had always admired David Watson's clearcut Christian faith, and had been helped by listening to his recorded sermons or reading his books, so I valued a chance to hear him talk about recent personal circumstances. I went back downstairs and fetched the radio, then plugged it into the bedroom wall socket in order to listen while setting my hair. The programme began with the beautiful, evocative hymn:

> Come down O Love divine,
> Seek Thou this soul of mine . . .

and then David spoke in a simple, moving way about his thoughts and reactions to so disturbing a diagnosis. I noticed his honest acceptance of the fact that no one could fully understand the mystery surrounding suffering, then the bold faith with which he declared his expectation of healing even though, following the discovery of liver secondaries, he had been given a poor prognosis.

The programme gripped my attention and I tried hard to enter into David's feelings of apprehension and bewilderment, only to find such close identification impossible. 'That's because there's no comparison between his situation and mine,' I realized as I switched off the radio. It was then, in complete contrast to such a conclusion, that I suddenly knew David's words *were* intensely rele-

vant to my own circumstances. It was as if Jesus had told
me, 'There is more for you in what you have heard than
you can fully grasp now.' That was all. No more than a
momentary 'inner knowing', yet it deeply disturbed me.
I could not cope with it so, reproving myself for even
entertaining such a possibility, I categorically dismissed
and forgot it.

Instead I went to fetch the smallest suitcase I could
find (it would give a brief-stay appearance when I walked
into the ward), and busied myself packing it, all the time
resenting the thought of being away from the family for
even so short a time. The surgeon had said, 'Ten days at
the most!'

Les sensed my sadness and late that night, as we knelt
together at the bedside, he prayed for me, putting into
calm steady words all the asking I wanted to express
myself, yet couldn't. My apprehension began to ease as I
lay back in bed, aware of the rich blessing of being comforted, particularly within the close strong bond of
marriage.

'Will you manage to sleep?' Les asked as we settled
down.

'Yes, but first I'll lie and listen to the river, just as I
always do.'

And as I lay and listened, I thought, 'There'll be no
more waiting now. No more days to count. Tomorrow it
will all start to happen, and then I can just look forward
to being home and completely well again.'

2

Pain and Joy

Such a strange week followed. Any hospital experience is an interweaving of fear and relief, sorrow and comfort. It is also the frustration of dependence and the luxury of being waited upon, the sadness of family separation and the pleasure of visits, flowers, cards. There's an unexpected loneliness in the midst of company, and an unusual capacity for sleep during daytime and wakefulness through long night hours, and all the while a yearning for the day when you can wear outdoor clothes, breathe fresh air, and think ordinary everyday thoughts again.

Several other patients were admitted that first day and there was the inevitable self-consciousness as, dressed in our new housecoats, we met around the dayroom lunch table. 'What did you say was wrong with you?' everyone seemed to be asking everyone else, while one or two long-standing patients offered sympathy and speculation about what was going to happen 'tomorrow when they take you downstairs to the theatre . . .'.

The long empty first evening was broken by the glad surprise of seeing Les again (he wasn't supposed to come until the following day). Then Mr H., an older friend from the city, came quietly in. It was so good of him to think of me! After we had talked for a while he prayed and I particularly valued that aspect of his visit. Jesus was right there with us even though I was finding it hard to recall his closeness amid such unfamiliar surroundings. Later my cheerful room-mate, Mrs D. (who was awaiting the same operation next day), beckoned me over to the window and we stood together watching as darkness enveloped the city streets and steeples, the office blocks and towering harbour derricks, reaching to the silver-grey sea beyond.

'This time tomorrow it will all be over!' Mrs D. reminded me with a quick smile. I valued her company, realizing that once the worst was over we'd be able to spur each other on to recovery. Last thing, before turning off the bedside light, I looked at the evening's verse in a daily reading leaflet I'd brought from home. It read: 'Leave all your worries with him, because he cares for you.' (1 Peter 5:7 GNB.)

I tried to leave my anxiety with the Lord but it was difficult. Fear kept thrusting back. Then I remembered Jesus' closeness and began to draw on the comforting awareness that I was not alone—nor would I ever be— and at last I fell asleep.

The next day every hour dragged. No drinks, no food, no further tests to be done. From early dawn the bustling ward routine continued, sweeping past and leaving me alone to think and then regret my thinking. Other patients called in to commiserate, giving detailed descriptions of their own operation experiences a few days earlier.

'They're sure to take you downstairs soon!' one of them said as the tea-time trays were carried in.

They had taken Mrs D. almost an hour before. 'Are they in the middle of her operation? Is she all right?' I kept wondering. At last the young theatre porter came to collect me, casually whistling his way in through the door. Though already sedated, I absorbed every detail: the long corridor and crowded lift, the swing of the heavy theatre block doors as they closed in, the glare of bright lights, the sickly smell of anaesthetics, the gentle reassuring voice. 'Just a small injection . . .' Then the sudden upsurge of suppressed apprehension, followed by a frightening plunge into total darkness.

*   *   *

Some time later there was the agony of gasping for air and then the immediate relief given by a rapidly applied oxygen mask, which smothered the embarrassing sound of my own involuntary groaning. Everything was muffled and blurred except for a few seconds, when I heard voices nearby, each word suddenly distinct.

'This patient, Mrs Brown, is ready to go back to the ward now. She's had a straightforward cholecystectomy, also a liver biopsy . . .'

The last four words stabbed into my thinking, clear, sharp, insistent. For those moments my mind was completely lucid and comprehending. 'Why a liver biopsy? Why . . .?' Then the darkness closed in.

Sometime, somewhere, I saw Les bending over me, and smelled the faint, exquisite scent of carnations.

'It's all over!' he whispered.

Oh, the immense relief! I tried to speak out my joy but the words wouldn't come. Only a hoarse, slow, unwanted question.

'Les, they said something about . . . about a liver biopsy. Why?'

He gripped my hand tightly. 'Did they? I don't know why. But you must sleep now. Just rest.'

For a few seconds more I tried to gaze up at him and saw the gentleness on his face. And the sudden concern. I tried to make my mind work further, determined to focus it away from my own need. Was Rachel there too? Was it her hand I could feel, stroking back my untidy hair? Were the boys all right at home? . . . then, gradually, painkillers blotted everything out. Deep welcome sleep and blessed forgetfulness of drips, tubes, awkward total dependence upon others. Forgetfulness even of my 'Why?'.

Each time I stirred there seemed to be a confusing intermingling of light and darkness. Nothing hung together. Every sound was distant and disconnected. Then another day began. The pain lessened and my mind became more clear. The reassuring pattern of morning,

afternoon and evening slowly returned. That night Mrs
D. eased herself up in bed and turned to smile at me.

'You feeling better? I'm nae bad!'

*   *   *

What bliss to be moving back to normality again—to get
up for the first time, walk a few steps, sit in a chair. On
the fifth day the drip needle was removed and I was free
to examine and rearrange my beautiful bouquet of pink
and red carnations, each one so perfect! Apart from
soreness I felt well. Amazingly well! All thought of the
biopsy had been thrust aside. 'Probably a routine procedure at every cholecystectomy,' I concluded and, since
the surgeon had made no mention of the matter, and he
was always frank with patients, there was no need for me
to think or speak about it either. It was obviously of no
consequence.

Now that the illness was completely over I could grasp
back my independence. No more episodes of pain. No
more dread of an operation. It was all past and gone.
Now I could simply look forward to becoming stronger
and stronger. What joy!

Sitting by the bed, I could watch the comings and
goings of staff members, particularly the two Marys.
There was Dr Mary, the house-surgeon, who had shown
particular understanding on my first day in hospital,
giving me time to express the pre-operative apprehension
which had been gathering in my mind.

'Do you have any questions? Can I help you?' she'd
asked, pausing to sit at the end of the bed. It had been
such a relief to put anxious thoughts into words and
then to hear Mary's reassuring explanations. The operation didn't seem nearly so big and threatening after
that.

Before leaving me that afternoon Mary had noticed a
Bible verse on a card someone sent me. Her face broke
into an immediate smile. 'Are you a Christian too?' And
we talked on for a few more minutes, sharing our pleasure at so happy and unexpected a discovery.

Then there was Mary, the first-year student nurse from West Africa, a young wife, and mother of a two-year-old daughter. Everyone warmed to Mary's easy, relaxed approach and her ready smile. Yet she had depth to her personality too. She cared instinctively *about* each patient (not merely for them), aware of needs without first having to be told. Mary also offered respite from our apprehension by making us laugh as we entered into her world of study books and lectures, babies' teething troubles and toddlers' birthday parties.

At last the ninth day came. 'Would you both like to go home? We need your beds!' the registrar explained. Would we *like* to? The very suggestion triggered huge excitement and Mrs D. and I dressed straightaway. Furthermore, this offered final confirmation of the fact that all was well. They wouldn't have been letting me go home otherwise. My mind was set completely at rest.

Mrs D. left soon after lunch and once she had gone I found it extra hard to wait until Les was free from his portering work at 5 p.m. By the time he came and found me sitting beside my small suitcase in the dayroom I was in tears. He couldn't think why. Neither could I, except that the hours until his coming had seemed so long. We drove home through the evening rush hour traffic. Then out along the April lanes, past the loch, the castle, the small steading where the twisted cherry tree was now in bud. Home to the empty High Street and the quiet riverside, to the two lads rushing out of the front door, 'Hallo Mum!'

'Now, don't you dare even to put your nose round the livingroom door!' Les commanded, scooping me quickly into his arms and carrying me up to the bedroom. 'There, the bed's warm and ready!'

I lay slowly back, gazing out at the green fields beyond the riverside beeches, where several ewes were grazing, surrounded by playful lambs. I could hear their faint, answering calls. What joy! What peace and stillness! I was home!

*   *   *

I thought it would be irksome to stay shut away in the bedroom for a week or so, but the very next day at least four visitors arrived. Our reassuring doctor and the district nurse, also our minister and a friend, Lorimer. He brought a large gloxinia plant with two deep red trumpet-shaped flowers already in bloom. Such a delight! In fact, every available space in the bedroom was filled with flowers, fruit, and more than fifty cards. I felt humbled to be on the receiving end of so much kindness, especially as it was impossible adequately to thank all who had shown such thoughtful concern.

It was good to be able to give extra time to the two lads too. They'd tackled their O-grade exams during my absence and now, lying across the bottom of the bed, were eager to talk about each paper. At least, Stuart was. Murray remained as silent as ever. He didn't even appear concerned about the long two-month wait until the results were posted, but I knew that, deep down, he cared about the outcome very much.

'It's going to be such a miserable drag waiting for the news, Mum!' Stuart moaned. 'I won't even be able to enjoy my summer with all that suspense hanging over me.'

And Les and I had the thought of April 30th hanging over us too. There had been no word of an interview result from the oil company. Just complete silence. 'So, if we don't hear from them by our deadline tomorrow, we'll go ahead and move south!' Les told me as we settled down late on the night of the 29th.

Within hours we'd *know* what we were doing! The long three-year drag of unemployment would be over at last. Completely resolved. I found it hard to go to sleep, I was so excited!

It was very misty across in the far field when we woke next day, but I could still hear the ewes calling and the high-pitched bleat of their lambs. After a leisurely Saturday morning mug of tea I found our place in the hymn book (we worked through it from cover to cover, taking one hymn a day). It was a paraphrase of Psalm 40 and, after singing the verses, we decided to read the

actual psalm in the *Good News Bible*. The words were apt,
stirring new hopefulness:

> I waited patiently for the Lord . . .
> and he listened to me . . .
> He set me safely on a rock
> and made me secure.
> He taught me to sing a new song,
> a song of praise to our God.

'Do you think the oil company's letter *will* come today?' I
asked Les later, as our time of quiet ended.

He frowned. 'Might do, I suppose. But it's only twelve
days since the interview. They said it could take three
weeks.'

Les got up and went down to prepare breakfast. As he
reached the bottom stair I strained my ears, hoping he
would pause by the doormat, finding that the letters had
already arrived. But there was no sound at all. Just a
long silence.

Then he called out, his voice steady as ever, 'It *has*
come!' I heard him slit the envelope open, then walk
slowly back up the stairs to me.

'Look at this!' he said, his expression unchanged.

It was a long letter beginning with 'We have pleasure
. . .' Oh, what a thrill! The company was making a firm
offer of a good, permanent post in the gas monitoring
department. And the answer had come on the very day
of our deadline! What more clearcut evidence of God's
leading did we need? Neither of us could find the right
words to say. We were too elated.

After reading right through the letter a second time
Les sat down on the bed and we praised God together,
using the previous day's hymn because we still couldn't
find our own words:

> We'll praise Him for all that is past
> and trust Him for all that's to come.

What a morning! What a day of celebration! Mrs G.

from down the road called just after breakfast. Although unaware of our sudden joy she had brought me a bouquet of daffodils and narcissi from her garden, each petal glistening with moisture. They were exquisite—and a very real part of our celebration that exciting morning. The lads were thrilled too (at least, we sensed that quiet Murray was) and Rachel hugged Les in delight when she arrived home on the morning bus. All day long there were happy exclamations as each new realization dawned upon the five of us:

Rachel: Mum, now you won't be moving away and leaving me all on my own in Aberdeen!

Stuart: That means I'll be able to finish my kartie at metalwork classes!

Murray: I'm glad I won't have to change schools again.

Then there was the long list of 'pending plans' which could now be brought into action.

'We can make and plant a side garden this summer,' I reminded Les over lunch.

'Yes, and maybe go ahead and start buying this house now the Council has suggested selling it off.'

One of the greatest thrills was being able to let friends and family members know. It was a delight to have good news to share at last, the answer to everyone's long, faithful praying.

'Won't Mother and Father be relieved!'

'We must tell Anne and Pete right away!'

'Yes, and don't forget Paul and Frances and Bob and . . .'

And the more phone calls Les made, the more our own joy increased, gathering further momentum.

Les's first call was to the mission leaders, and after hearing about the oil company's offer they were immediately pleased for us, convinced this was God's answer. 'The work will start in a month's time,' I heard Les explain over and over again to relatives and friends. There was already a distinct lightness and ease about him, as if he had just tossed a huge burden aside and watched, with incredulous delight, as it rolled down a long weary slope and out of sight for ever.

My thoughts began to reach out into the weeks ahead
before Les's new work began, and I remembered the
three youngsters were going away for a youth weekend
in mid-May.

'Shall we plan a short break then too?' I suggested to
Les.

'Yes, let's!'

So we booked in at a small guest house up on the
northern coast at Nairn, glad of an opportunity to be
alone together and regear our thinking in eager anticipation of the future.

*   *   *

It was the happiest of weekends. We drove north one
Friday evening, as soon as Les finished his portering,
and arrived in Nairn just before sunset.

'Let's buy a Chinese takeaway meal and eat it by the
shore!' I suggested, so we took containers of sweet-sour
pork and rice (I was able to eat such things by now)
down to the beach and sat in the car looking out over the
Moray Firth. The tide was receding, its waves gently
fingering the weed-covered rocks, while away on the far
side of the estuary a pale sun was scattering fragments
of silver across the calm water. We left the remains of
our rice for a line-up of squabbling gulls and drove to
the nearby guest house. It was good to be there again,
almost a year after our previous stay. Darkness was
falling but the garden was still bright with Maytime
colour—tulips, grape hyacinths, narcissi, polyanthus,
daffodils, pansies—and just above, a few large herring
gulls wheeled and called against the blue-black sky. I
paused by the side gate, listening to their echoing cries
and delighting in the smell of fresh salty air.

Next day Les drove me east along the coastline. Vivid
golden gorse lined the lanes on our way to Findhorn,
matched by clumps of dandelions on the sheltered grass
below. Wild cherries were in blossom too, scattering
their delicate white petals as we passed. We stopped at
the Findhorn jetty for a while, watching a yachtsman

struggling to hoist a resistant mainsail on his way to the
open sea. Further east, at Lossiemouth, the harbour was
crowded with moored trawlers, and at the quayside several small boys were noisily trying to outdo one another
with their fishing casts, while a black and white collie
kept darting back and forth between them, breathless
with excitement at his part in the confusion.

After this picnic-time entertainment we drove inland,
reaching Pluscarden by mid-afternoon. It was a large,
prominent abbey set in the valley beneath a high ridge
of hills, and peaceful with birdsong. We walked up the
winding driveway in silence, almost in awe, and hesitantly
pushed at the tall, heavy door of the chapel.

As it creaked open we heard the solemn sound of
plainsong and realized that the brothers must be at one
of their afternoon offices, so we sat and listened as the
music rose to echo through the high stone arches. A
magnificent sound, awesome and yet uplifting, as if we
had been suddenly brought right into Christ's majestic
presence. Such an awareness took me far on beyond the
personal trauma of recent months into a new, vivid
appreciation of Jesus' splendour. He was so great, yet at
the same time, through his Holy Spirit, so graciously
involved with each individual. Even with me. I sensed
that, in tenderness, he had particularly planned those
few moments and I longed for the singing to go on and
on. But soon the short afternoon office came to an end
and the brothers began to file out in their flowing cream-
coloured robes, leaving the chapel to its silence.

On our way back to the car we bought a jar of Pluscarden honey at the small shop, and then drove on
along the narrow empty road. It began to rise steadily to
cross the high ridge beyond the abbey and all the way
the larches stretched out their new, intensely green
shoots towards us. Les stopped the car while a farm
tractor passed and I caught sight of several frail wood
anemones scattered like stars in the soft grass beside a
bubbling burn. Later, at the summit of the ridge, we left
the car and gazed out over the wide spread of land and
sand and sea far below, letting each detail become fixed,

with joy, in our minds. Then, finally, we drove back to Nairn via Brodie and Cawdor castles. It had been a wonderfully refreshing day.

*   *   *

Once home again I began to feel much stronger and, indifferent to a continuing weight loss, set my mind to all kinds of plans for the immediate future. What about another writing project now that the manuscript on suffering and bereavement had at last been accepted? Maybe, too, we could buy a better carpet for the downstairs living area and I could then sew curtains and cushion covers to match? And what shrubs should we choose for the newly-dug side border? All these questions filled my mind with pleasure and eager anticipation as summer moved in across our quiet north-eastern corner. I started cycling again too, gradually trying out longer routes through the nearby Fetternear woods, or beyond the golf course towards the cluster of cottages at Craigearn. It gave me immense pleasure to be mobile on two wheels once again and I made a point of waving to friends in passing so that they would see how well I was progressing.

Towards the end of May, Les and Murray dug over the vegetable patch and planted several packets of seeds: carrots, beetroots, peas, radishes, lettuce. As we sat down for lunch that day (the back door still wide open to let in the fresh warm sunlight), Les stopped to ask God for a good harvest. The strawberry plants were already doing well, having grown into quite a thicket despite a complete lack of cosseting. Odd that they should so thrive in a chilly northern climate.

And so summer came, completing our eager expectation and delight. How I loved its rich significance! The dark winter had long since passed, forgotten amid our certainty of joy.

3

Sting in the Tail

The days grew hotter and hotter. 'Summer has now begun!' a news broadcast proclaimed as May drew to a close.

My final post-operative check was due during the last week of the month and as the date coincided with a school holiday, Murray joined me on the trip into the city. En route we noticed a skylark perched on the warm tarmac at the roadside, so stopped to study it at close quarters. I had not realized skylarks were such ordinary looking birds, but what a song! 'Surely no one could ever grow tired of listening to it!' I commented happily to Murray as we drove on, and the mirror reflected his answering smile. The sight of the skylark added an extra touch of pleasure to the occasion. It was to be my very last appointment with the surgeon.

There was time to spare when we reached the city so Murray helped with some shopping before setting off for a favourite model shop.

'I need the steering gear for that new yacht,' he explained as we parted at a crossroads.

I walked lightly on down the hot, dusty side-street and into the cool, echoing clinic, all the time reminding myself, 'This is my last time here!' because the thought gave such satisfaction.

The waiting room was half full and many of the patients looked tense and apprehensive. I felt for them. 'Probably here on their first visit,' I guessed, 'and dread-

ing what the surgeon's going to say.' The tea trolley
came round but I couldn't face a hot drink on so stifling
a day, so instead chose the least-torn magazine from a
pile on the table and settled down to study the recipe
page.

'Mrs Brown?' the nurse was looking enquiringly
around the rows of waiting patients, and I jumped up in
response. She led me to one of the examination rooms.
'You're not a new patient, are you?'

'Oh no! In fact, this is my final visit,' I told her, and
she smiled. 'That's nice! But you'd better undress and
get up on the couch all the same. Part of the routine, you
know.'

I lay there for a long time, waiting for the surgeon to
come, and while I did so relaxed in the peacefulness of
the cool white room.

Voices sounded in the corridor outside. The surgeon
and his registrar came slowly in.

'Hallo, how are you doing Elaine?' (I liked the way
they used my first name.)

'Very well! You'll be pleased with me, I'm sure!' And I
grinned confidently up at them.

The surgeon didn't respond. Instead he pulled a chair
close to the couch and sat down, letting his fingers run
lightly over the well-healed scar.

'I'm afraid there's been a "sting in the tail" to your
operation . . .'

I caught my breath. 'Yes? . . .'

He told me that during the operation they'd found a
very small, seemingly insignificant liver growth. Subsequent laboratory tests had revealed it to be malignant,
although the results had not come through until after
I'd left hospital.

'. . . I'm very sorry, but I need to operate again and
take away some more of the surrounding tissue, just to
be on the safe side.'

My whole world suddenly seemed to cave in. I was
completely overwhelmed. Yet, far away in the distance, I
heard myself calmly agreeing and asking, 'When?'

'As soon as we can arrange a bed for you. It won't be a

big operation this time, you'll only need to be in hospital
for four or five days. I'm just sorry this has happened.
We don't know the cause, even though we've looked
right through your notes for possible clues. It's a rare
type of primary growth, occurring mostly in tropical
countries, which is why we didn't recognize the problem
straight away.'

                    *   *   *

The surgeon could not have been more kind or understanding, giving me as much time as possible on his busy
out-patient afternoon. I sensed that he and the registrar
were feeling for me, which was comforting, but my
thoughts were still in utter confusion. Somehow I dressed
and gathered up my shopping bags, but I hardly knew
how to walk out of the clinic door, past the waiting
patients, and into the street beyond. The surgeon
watched me go. 'We'll see you soon!' he called out sym-
pathetically. Did he notice the tears I was trying so hard
to hide?

The street was still sunlit, the dusty air still heavy and
hot. Pigeons were strutting along the dirty flagstones,
pecking at litter, and people kept hurrying past, faces
flushed and damp with perspiration. Nothing had
changed, yet everything was completely different. I
couldn't think which direction to take. Where had I left
the car? Where was Murray? Eventually I made my way
down the cobbled side-street towards the model shop,
but he had gone. I found him at last, leaning up against
the car in the shadowy underground car park, the bag
of steering gear hanging out of his jeans' pocket.

I took the quickest route away from the city. It led
past Loch Skene, and all the way back I deliberately
focused on the beauty spread out in every direction,
aware of a sudden desperate hunger for perfection in
order to counteract all the inner confusion. Driving
slowly, I absorbed every detail of that peaceful summer
scene: the far hills, intensely green in the sunlight, the
loch sparkling beneath a gleaming sky, two colourful

cock pheasants strolling between the deep furrows of a
roadside field. I looked and looked, finding brief comfort and an easing of the turmoil. Murray sat in silence
behind me and I appreciated his company, though said
nothing to him, apart from commenting on the loveliness
of the day and the brilliance of the cock pheasant's
feathers against the brown earth. He nodded, quick to
enter into my enjoyment.

As soon as we reached home Murray went to fit the
steering parts to his yacht while I made two large mugs
of tea. Looking out of the kitchen window I noticed
swifts skimming the sky, so took my drink out to the
garden seat and sat studying them. So many birds, and
all sizes too! It was my first sighting of swifts that summer
and their return was always a thrill. Did they really
remain in the sky for two years after fledging, returning
to earth only when nesting for the first time? I gazed at
the row of tall scarlet tulips lining our back pathway,
petals wide open to the sun. I gazed at the river, the sky,
the slow drifting clouds. And all the while I was thinking,
'It hasn't happened. They made a mistake. Or maybe I
misunderstood?'

At last I went indoors. It was time to sort out the
shopping and make a start on supper preparations. But
first, sensing an acute need for Jesus' help, I wanted to
try to put all my bewildered thoughts into some sort of
prayer, so I sank down on one of the diningroom chairs
to ask for his immediate help. The distress was growing.
I hardly knew what to do or say.

It was then, when starting to plead for Christ's strength,
that something totally unexpected happened. Suddenly,
unmistakably, the Holy Spirit intervened, giving me a
compelling new awareness of the good things which
were still mine to enjoy despite the overwhelming shock.
Just as the ordered loveliness that afternoon had been a
solace, so the gratitude which sprung from such beauty
now began to offer a further measure of calm. I found
myself praising Jesus over and over again for each touch
of his love and tenderness. For the beauty spread out so
lavishly around me, for the sunlit summer's day, and

then, too, for the surgeon's kindness and skilled help,
for the fact that I would be going back to a hospital ward
I already knew, and most of all for the assurance of it
being only a small operation next time, with a good
outlook afterwards. ('The problem isn't likely to spread,'
the surgeon had told me.) As I lingered there beside the
table I began to recognize such praise as Jesus' wise,
entirely appropriate gift to me. It was his way of offering
the help for which I had pleaded. A totally unexpected
way.

It was time to cook the supper. Murray had already
been in to raid the biscuit tin, and Stuart would soon be
arriving from school, hungry as ever. I laid the table and
set out some bread and a chocolate sponge, then cooked
our cheese omelettes. Les arrived home at 6 p.m.

'Everything all right at the clinic?' he asked, almost as
soon as he came in at the door. I went to welcome him
with a kiss, avoiding his questioning glance. 'I'll tell you
about it later.'

When the washing up was finished we sat out on the
garden seat—the evening sun still warm as its long rays
slanted down through the woodland beeches—and I
briefly explained what the surgeon had said. Les responded calmly, quietly, just as he always did, yet I hated
having to spell out the few facts. I couldn't bear for Les
to hear such news just when there had been so much
deep joy and relief to delight in together. How could
this have happened? And why now, when I was so full of
confidence, so sure I would never have to go back to the
hospital again? For some reason the last fact stung most
of all. I couldn't bear for my certainty of healing and the
pleasure of renewed strength to be suddenly undermined.
I couldn't face going right back again to thinking about
hospital admission, an operation, convalescence, etc. It
had all been over. Completely finished. I was well again.
'I *am* well again! I am!' In desperation I tried to combat
the rising distress with such insistence, but it was useless.
The distress had grown too strong.

'Please, Lord, please help me,' I cried within myself. 'I
just can't go through with this. I can't even believe it has

STING IN THE TAIL

happened.'

All these thoughts went round and round in my mind as Les and I stayed on in the quiet garden. I couldn't put my anguish into words. Maybe I didn't need to. Les understood. I began to draw on the comfort of being with him, the relief of having shared the surgeon's words. When it grew cold we went back indoors. The scarlet tulip petals had folded and closed, but the swifts were still skimming back and forth across the sky.

By eleven o'clock night had fallen and the house was silent. My thoughts had grown calmer but it was impossible to sleep. Why did this happen just when everything had started to go so well? Just when our long night had ended? Why? Hadn't we faced enough setbacks? I felt the tears rush back and tried to stop them, determined to hide my shock from Les in order to minimize the inevitable overshadowing of our recent happiness. Then I began deliberately to listen for the gentle murmuring of the Don. (The water level was now low and the river's voice very soft.) 'Old Nog', one of our resident herons, must have been standing somewhere on the far bank, for I heard him give a couple of loud squawks which echoed through the further woods. Was he waiting for the silver flash of a fish rising above the moonlit water? At last I felt myself growing drowsy, worn out by my thoughts. The acute inner pain was lessening and I realized, with relief, that at least it was *my* problem this time. I wouldn't have to stand by, helplessly watching someone else in the family suffer. That would have been far harder.

It was a long night. I kept half waking only to be confronted full on with a mental replay of the previous day's events. Then, with a rush of unwilling recognition, I recalled David Watson's broadcast and the strange inner 'knowing' which had come to me afterwards. My mind went back to the theatre sister's words and her reference to a liver biopsy. All at once the connection struck with frightening reality. I could no longer forget such incidents, or consider them of no significance. In giving them, God had wanted me to come gradually to this present point so that the final realization would then be easier to bear. But I had not wanted to listen or understand, and instead had turned away from the offer of any such fore-knowing.

Lying there in the half-darkness I could only feel amazed that God should have tried to help me in such a clearcut way, and the thought was unexpectedly reassuring. It indicated he had had the matter in hand all along. As before, nothing was unanticipated, everything had been foreseen and therefore provided for. Perhaps, in offering those two pre-glimpses, he had wanted me to come to him for safe refuge, rather than to recoil in immediate disbelief?

*   *   *

It was a relief to see the first silvery streaks of dawn reaching far out across the sky. A little while later several noisy jackdaws began to glide past our window en route to their daily breakfast feast at a neighbouring bird table. I was glad to get up as the eager sun rose higher into the sky. Miss Puss, impatient for food, was already running her claws down the leg of the old oak sideboard downstairs, determined to arouse a swift, if irritated, response.

By 8.30 a.m. Les and the lads had left for work and school, and the house became uncomfortably silent. I decided to wash the livingroom windows and launder the net curtains in order to escape my thoughts. It didn't work. Every detail of the situation kept going back and forth across my mind, rubbing a deeper groove. I sensed the danger of being taken over by such circumstances yet it was so difficult to break free. 'If only I could go back to this time yesterday and play the day over again, making it completely different,' I thought, remembering the words I had been so sure the surgeon would say—'You're doing fine! No need to come back again!' Oh, why couldn't it have been that way?

'It won't be nearly so bad this time,' I kept telling myself. But then last time there had been no sinister aspect to the matter. This time there was, even if minimal. I didn't know how to handle it, how to cope. 'Would Helen be able to help?' The idea came as I was hanging out the last dripping curtain. What a blessing to have a nearby doctor friend you could phone at (almost) any time! I dialled her number and then settled into the chair beside the telephone. Surely she'd be there! Or was it her day for duty at the health centre? The ringing tone went on and on. Just as I was about to put the receiver down Helen answered.

'Sorry, I was giving the children a picnic elevenses on the lawn!'

It was a great relief to share my thoughts with Helen. All the while I found myself reaching out desperately for any reassurance she could give. Would Helen say, 'It's just a small thing!' Would she take a casual approach? I so much wanted her to do so. But Helen was silent at first, then she spoke with gentle understanding, saying how sorry she was to hear the news.

'We'll be praying specially for you,' she promised, and I drew strength from the calmness of her voice. How *could* she have taken a casual, 'Never mind, it will all be all right!' approach? After putting the phone down I realized it was unreasonable even to have expected such a response.

Miss Puss was weaving in and out of the bucket and cloths when I returned to the window-cleaning. Then she leapt on to the narrow sill, getting her long black tail pinched when a sudden gust of wind shut the window. I quickly released her and she jumped, still growling, into the street outside, her fur fluffed in confused embarrassment. Karen, a close neighbour, was passing, holding her small daughter, Kirsty, in her arms.

'My, hasn't she grown!' I called, then went out of the front door to admire the laughing baby.

'Are you keeping better now?' Karen asked, glancing at me with concern.

'Yes,' I answered quickly, then changed the subject. 'Isn't this heat wave marvellous! And I love Kirsty's new sun bonnet!'

After lunch I took a small, favourite book out onto the
garden seat, and sat in the cool shade of the wide eaves.
It was a very old edition of Maria Ridley Havergal's
compilation *Memorials,* recently lent by a friend, Thea,
'because I know you love the way F.R.H. thinks and
writes!' I had been reading a few pages each day and
that afternoon came across a sentence full of meaning:
'More pain . . .? May it be more support, more grace,
more tenderness, from the God of all comfort, more
and more! May we not expect the 'mores' to be in tender
proportion to each other?'*

I read the words over several times, absorbing their
offered strength. Jesus was so carefully and deliberately
reaching out to comfort my sadness.

And I was helped in a similar way later when I walked
up the road to visit a close friend, Anne, for our weekly
time of prayer together. On the way I determined to
take myself in hand and not allow circumstances to throw
me into such confusion, so when Anne asked about the
previous day's appointment I explained the facts calmly
and objectively. Was she shocked? I didn't know. Outwardly Anne was quiet and hesitant, handling me with
care. We prayed together for a few minutes and such a
sharing helped to quieten my mind.

'Thank you, Lord, for friends like Helen and Anne
who've already helped to lift the weight a little,' I found
myself saying as I walked on from Anne's house towards
the village.

For a few moments I began to look at my problem in a
new way, seeing it as a very small thing indeed when set
in the total context of our lives, both here and in the
eternity beyond. 'What will it matter then, when we go
on to live in an entirely different and immense dimension?' The realization, though fleeting, offered balance
to my thinking. Then I forced myself to look outwards,
in order to concentrate on the needs of other people I
knew. What about Sally, still caught in a tight tangle of
mental despair? Or Annette, and the ongoing uncer-

* Frances Ridley Havergal from Maria Ridley Havergal (ed.) *Memorials*
(James Nisbet & Co 1882).

tainty with which, following her operation, she must now live? And then there was Euan's long, seemingly insoluble problem with alcoholism too. Could I understand a little more now? Feeling *with* them rather than merely for them? My mind began to focus particularly on a young teenager, Michael, who'd been found to have cancer the previous year. At the time I had been concerned but hardly involved. It was someone else's problem, not mine. But now the frightening truth turned to fling itself straight at me. I'd got it too. It was my problem as well. 'But it's only a very small matter with me. Nothing at all,' I quickly insisted.

There were a few other people around me now, all of us heading for the High Street shops. I began to worry about how to share what had happened with village friends. Just three weeks ago they had so eagerly entered with us into the gladness of Les's new job. I couldn't bear for my own circumstances to undermine that pleasure and yet I didn't want to be evasive (as with Karen that morning), lest such avoidance should lead friends to think it was an unmentionable matter in which I didn't want or need their help. To take that line would be to risk hurting them and would also eventually increase my own distress.

'The more you open yourself out to others when faced with serious illness, the more you talk about it, the better it will be for you and also for them. In this way a person finds release.'

I had put those words together for the book manuscript only a few months earlier, and there was much else in a similar vein. So easy to write in comfortable impersonal theory, so hard to live out in the pain of a real-life situation. It now seemed ironic that I could have been writing that book, trying to project myself into circumstances which were totally unfamiliar. Such a projection was all but impossible, for how could anyone really know except through exacting personal experience? Not that I was thinking of my own situation in terms of serious illness, far less in terms of death. I expected to be given an excellent prognosis once the small operation

had been carried out. 'I must concentrate on that certainty,' I kept urging myself, 'excluding every other possibility.' How I longed to get the surgery over and finished quickly. How many more days would I have to wait?
Would they find a bed within the next week?

All these different thoughts kept going through my
mind as I neared the shops. Hazel, a village friend,
passed me at the bank corner, trailing young Fiona
home from the supermarket.

'How are you getting on now?' she asked, setting her
heavy carrier bags down on the pavement.

'Very well, except that . . .' I hesitated, afraid to go on.
'Except that I have to go back into hospital.'

'Oh, I am sorry. Why? Is it the same problem again?'

'Well no, not exactly.'

I forced myself to tell Hazel briefly what had happened,
all the time playing down facts, wanting them to sound
almost trivial. Hazel didn't know how to respond and I
felt for her.

'Don't worry, I'll soon be bouncing around again!' I
said, rushing into the awkward silence, and then chang-
ing the subject. 'Don't let me keep you standing here on
this windy corner. Fiona will be wanting her "jeelie piece"
for tea!'

'I'll be thinking of you,' Hazel said quietly, then she
picked up her carrier bags, took Fiona's hand, and walked
slowly on down the road.

It took a long time to complete the shopping. I couldn't
concentrate on the list, and then there was quite a queue
in the post office as it was family allowance day. I was
glad to chat to another friend, Aileen, while waiting.
She'd heard about Les's job.

'Please give him my congratulations,' she instructed.
'He'll enjoy working for the company. I was a secretary
there before the children came along.'

Outside the door I passed a neighbour, Isobel, posting a pile of business letters, and we walked part of the
way home together. She was as full of laughter as ever
and I was soon laughing too. Isobel always saw things in
such an easy-going, lighthearted way and as she chatted

on I sensed the importance of staying open to fun in order to be taken right out of myself. Isobel didn't ask any questions so I didn't need to refer to myself at all. Instead, by reacting readily to her humour, I could temporarily forget that anything was wrong. It was refreshing.

We parted at the last turning and I decided to make a short detour along the river bank before going home. It was so peaceful there. House-martins were gliding low over the grass and, nearby, a chaffinch was singing out his clear, complicated tune. Clumps of white cow parsley were just in flower, also a few gleaming gold celandines and a patch of greater stitchwort. The broom bushes, though still somewhat shabby after winter gales, were about to burst into bloom and all the wild roses were in leaf. How much it meant to linger amid such beauty!

But I was glad to reach the house at last and put down the heavy shopping bags. Murray had just come in from school and Miss Puss was lavishing affection upon him in the hope of being served an early supper. I caught sight of a carefully wrapped bouquet lying on the dining table. Who was it for? Where had it come from?

'That wifey friend of yours just brought it,' Murray muttered, spooning a generous helping of cat food into Miss Puss's dish.

'Which wifey?'

'You know, the one who lives near the school.'

'You mean my friend Hazel?'

'Yes, maybe that's what you call her.'

I peeped inside the paper wrappings and found several sprays of white and pale yellow carnations, fresh and sweetly fragrant. What a joy! And to think that Hazel, with her limited income and a large family to feed, had gone to the expense and effort of quickly buying and delivering that bouquet to me. I felt very moved. The flowers were such a beautiful expression of the care which lay behind so costly a gift.

Fetching a pottery jug from the china cabinet, I sat down straight away and began to arrange the carnations, studying the small fragrant blooms in detail. Each was

exquisite! It took a long time to fill the vase but the delay
was deliberate. Once more I felt a need to satisfy the
continuing inner hunger for beauty and perfection. It
was not something I could express in words, for I had
never experienced such a yearning before. I only knew
that, by focusing on simple loveliness, I would find an
important balance for my growing apprehension. In
recognizing that there was still purpose and order in the
beauty with which I was surrounded, my frail faith was
reassured. Was there a similar wise, ordered purpose
even in my own suffering?

Hazel's gift was of particular help, offering calm as
the day ended. The inner pain started to lessen and,
though aware it would surge back, I was grateful for the
respite. There *was* still so much cause for gratitude!

'Lord, thank you for your tenderness to me. For still
being there even when, in my anxiety, I've ignored or
forgotten you. Thank you that genuine laughter and
pleasure are still possible because they come from beyond
myself as your appropriate, much-needed gifts.'

*   *   *

Next day the postman brought a letter from the oil
company, giving further details about Les's employment.
The starting date had been fixed for June 6th and training for the job would take place during the first month.

'You've only another fortnight to wait!' I reminded
Les when he came in from work, and he grinned back. It
was good to have those work plans to consider and I
kept plying Les with questions, asking him to explain
various details, as a way of escaping from thinking about
myself. It gave me particular pleasure to picture Les in
his new work, dressed in a smart shirt and tie instead of
the older clothes needed for portering. What a relief for
him to have permanent work at last, just like most of the
other men along our road. No more uncomfortable self-
consciousness when the topic of unemployment crept
into conversation. No more miserable awareness of being
in the jobless minority while everyone else set off for a

busy day's work. No more embarrassment at having to ask a neighbour to sign the fortnightly benefit application form. No more frustration at being unable to provide personally for basic family needs. That was completely over. We could leave it all behind.

I kept thinking of this, feeling a deep gladness for Les. We had waited so long for this answer, yet how much more valuable it had become for the waiting. As I deliberately concentrated on these different aspects of Les's situation I began to feel grateful because this particular family pleasure had occurred at such a time. Up to this point I had repeatedly objected, 'Why has my illness come to overshadow the joy?' but now I was more willing to see circumstances the other way round: one special purpose of the joy was that it should be a means of easing my inner sorrow.

We were sitting round the supper table with the two boys when Les unexpectedly said, 'Mum has to go back into hospital. They've found that a small lump they took away last time was malignant, so it's best if they remove a little more tissue.'

The two of them stopped eating.

'Sorry Mum!' Stuart turned to me, frowning in immediate sympathy. Murray sat still, looking at his plate, saying nothing at all. I knew he cared deep down.

As the long week ended I waited anxiously for a letter from the hospital, but it didn't come.

'There'll be word on Monday,' I told myself, then went back to the usual housekeeping routine. Though careful to appear calm, I was inwardly numbed and shocked, still unable to believe what had happened. It seemed impossible. Our minister's wife had telephoned earlier in the week to say how sorry she was about the news.

'You'll be feeling shocked,' Mary had said, and I appreciated her frank insight. It was helpful to hear another person putting my confused thoughts into a clearcut category.

'It's quite normal to react in such a way,' Mary went on, with understanding. 'After a few days you'll begin to

come to terms with what has happened, but not yet.'
How good it was of Mary to phone and talk at length
with me. Her reassurance kept coming back into my
mind, particularly her comment that a delay in admission
could only be interpreted as encouraging. 'They'd have
taken you into hospital straight away if it was really
serious!' she'd remarked, and that certainly was true. So
I could be further reassured.

On the Sunday morning a friend, Marion, came up to
me after church. She must have heard about my problem
for I noticed her brief awkwardness as she searched for
the right words.

'I'm so sorry,' she said at last, and tears came to her
eyes. It moved me to see such concern. Few people were
prepared actually to 'weep with those who weep'. I was
becoming vividly aware of the strong, supportive empathy with which people had begun to surround me.
How much this meant! What a difference it made!

That same afternoon Les suggested a drive along the
Lord's Throat road. We parked at the forestry centre
(now hot and dusty in the summer sunshine) and walked
up the favourite woodland path. Soon we came across a
first common dog violet half hidden by tall new grass,
and several delicate wood sorrel flowers clustered near
the burn. I appreciated the clear, fresh air, the stillness
of those fragrant pine woods. Everything was the same
—ordered, beautiful, calm. No happening in my small
world could alter that quiet loveliness. It would always
be the same, always an offered refuge for me.

When we reached home I caught sight of a new bloom
on the gloxinia plant Lorimer had given. A trumpet of
deep red, shading to scarlet, and then rimmed with
pink, the edge delicately serrated. 'Fantastic!' Les exclaimed when I put it right in the centre of the supper
table.

Murray's eyes lit up too. I had a feeling that all along
he had been watching the tight green bud push doggedly
up through its thick canopy of leaves.

4

Is *God Good?*

Les stopped his portering work a week before the new employment was due to begin, so we could enjoy a few days together. On the Monday of his holiday we went into the city to choose a new carpet for our large living area, and on the way called in at the hospital for a coffee date with Rachel. She met us at the small cafeteria close to the main entrance.

'We want to share something with you,' Les said, as soon as he had brought three plastic beakers of steaming coffee to the table. Rachel looked up at him with an eager smile.

'Yes?'

'Mum will be going back into the ward here . . .'

Rachel's eyes widened with concern as Les went on to give the few details.

'Mum, I'm sorry,' she said gently, touching my arm. 'But I'll come and see you as often as I can. You know that, don't you?'

I loved her the more for her daughterly concern.

'Yes . . . and we can have fun looking through magazines together and chatting about all the crazy things you've been getting up to!'

Our coffee date ended cheerfully. The light-hearted cover-up was helpful.

'See you at the weekend!' Rachel called as she walked away down the corridor in her smart uniform slacks and tunic.

The carpet warehouse, down by the harbour, was a fascinating, rambling place. Tucked away at the top of three flights of narrow wooden stairs, its old plank flooring was laden with rack upon rack of carpeting, all colours and qualities. We walked up and down the rows considering various patterns, while an attentive salesman hovered close by, adding encouraging comments. One pattern particularly caught my eye, but the salesman shook his head.

'I'm afraid that length looks too short for your large room.' So the search started all over again, but there was no suitable alternative.

'Wait a minute,' the salesman insisted, seeing my disappointment, and he cleared other customers away from a large area of uneven floorboards, before instructing a couple of assistants to unwind and measure the first carpet. Despite its low cost it looked impressive laid out on the shabby warehouse floor, and it was four inches *over* the required length. So we brought the carpet home in triumph and Murray and Les spent all afternoon fitting it, much to Miss Puss's disgust. At the first hint of furniture removals she fled upstairs to shelter under our bedspread where she imagined herself to be totally invisible, and therefore invulnerable.

The carpet purchase called for a celebration supper so I busied myself making the lads' favourite lasagne and then, just before serving up, took time off to admire the new-look living area. The carpet was just right! A pleasing tile pattern in red, beige and black. What a good day it had been! And later, as everyone tucked in to the meal (even I, for the recent nausea had eased considerably), I realized carpet-buying offered its own important therapeutic value.

'Now for some home-made cushion covers to match!' I told Les.

*   *   *

On the first day of June I woke to hear a blackbird singing at 3.30 a.m.! It seemed to be his way of welcoming our midsummer month and I wondered if he had slept at all. The nights never really grew dark now, and the brief summer was so much appreciated in the north. I always loved it and yet, this time, my joy was mingled with sadness as the beautiful month began. If only I could break free. As the blackbird sang on into the growing dawn light I thought back to the beginning of May. Everything had been so exciting then. 'Remember the Nairn weekend?' I reflected. 'Remember the solemn, awesome beauty of Pluscarden? The thrill of seeing spring unfold as we entered into all its eager hopefulness?'

Such memories accentuated the sorrow of present circumstances and, in the early morning stillness, all the facts burst back across my mind, every detail more vivid and disturbing. I pictured the small white room in the out-patient's clinic and heard the surgeon's words all over again. How many more times would I relive that experience? How much longer would I try to dismiss the problem, all the while knowing I must ultimately face and accept it? But I couldn't accept. I couldn't be at peace. Every instinct rebelled against illness, weakness, temporary dependence, and particularly against the sinister aspect of the situation, however slight it might be. Over and over again I had tried to persuade myself, 'It's only small. It doesn't matter.' But, for all that, it did matter. I was determined to resist and fight.

By now an additional fear had begun to grip me. Suppose, by the partial removal of suspicious tissue, the problem had already been seeded elsewhere? This fear now began to override the rest, making me feel as if some evil alien thing was already reaching slowly out across my body. How could I be at peace? How could I passively accept? When Les woke I tried to put this new fear into words so that, by sharing it, I would find relief. Maybe he'd just say, 'Oh, I'm sure a spread hasn't occurred. No need to worry!' But he didn't. (If he had expressed such a view, would I have been convinced anyway?) He only said, 'Let's leave it with the surgeon. He'll take good care of the whole matter.'

All of this was an over-reaction of course. I had allowed

fear to swell to unreasonable proportions, forgetting that it always tended to such an exaggeration unless deliberately checked. But this time it had taken over even before I'd been aware of what was happening, making any such check much more difficult. Deep down, too, I sensed that my way of checking fear— evasion— was only delaying the needed facing and quiet acceptance of circumstances. Such a confrontation, followed by deliberate relinquishment, must come. But I was not nearly ready yet. The whole thing was still too raw. For the moment I could only cling to what was becoming increasingly important—a frequent, deliberate concentration on other things, the needs of other people. I needed to go on lingering with them all, for only then could I find genuine relief. It was almost as if, by doing so, I caught glimpses of some faint creative purpose in suffering which kept beckoning me on beyond the present confusion.

The hospital letter arrived later that morning. My admission date was to be in a week's time. I filled in the enclosed form and put it ready for the post, then sat down to compile several more lists, as well as reminders to Les about paying the milkman, collecting bus fare change for Stuart, and dinner money for Murray, etc.

'Don't worry, we'll manage fine!' Les insisted when he saw slips of paper piling up around me. He didn't understand my need to be extra busy.

'It helps to have plenty to do,' I told him, but he just gave me a puzzled frown.

Karen called in later to ask if Les could change the battery of their car. (Her husband was away on an offshore oil rig.) We chatted for a while, then Karen commented, 'I hear you're going back into hospital?' This time it was more important to make a more appropriate response to her questioning approach.

'Yes, they need to operate again.'

'Oh, is something still wrong?'

I explained the whole story lest Karen should feel I was shrouding the matter in deliberate silence, or avoiding it by giving only half the facts. It was irksome to have to go over the account again, but the full truth needed to be out in the open. Even so I couldn't bring myself to use the word 'cancer'. Saying it had become acutely uncomfortable to me even though, in nursing days, the problem had been commonly and easily discussed. Now it was quite different. Direct personal involvement had completely altered my response. Cancer had become a disturbing word, at least for the moment. One day, when everything was over, I might be able to use it easily again.

Karen listened carefully but said nothing at all, apart from, 'Let me know how it all goes, won't you?'. I could tell she was afraid to respond in the wrong way, so had chosen carefully to sidestep, and I understood. Had our roles been reversed I would probably have struggled for the right words too. It was strange to have become rather an enigma to the friends and neighbours who were aware of the problem. Yet, although unsure as to how to handle the matter, they had not in any way avoided me, in fact I sensed an unspoken concern and sympathy which brought considerable comfort.

All the same, I had recently grown very self-conscious, an unwelcome feeling never experienced to such a degree before. What were people thinking when I passed them in the street? Had friends noticed I'd become thinner and that it was harder now to keep up my usual easy-going smile? I decided to counteract this uncomfortable self-awareness by making more of an effort to look smart, so altered clothes until they fitted reasonably well, and made a point of having my hair neatly cut and permed.

'Wow, you look completely different, Mum!' Rachel exclaimed the moment I arrived home after a Saturday morning at the village hairdressers. 'I'd have walked past you in the street!'

*   *   *

Heavy rain fell as Les's holiday week ended, and I woke one morning to hear large heavy drops hammering against the window pane, but the blackbird was singing as usual, quite unconcerned. Always now my first thoughts were filled with dread of the hospital but this time I forcibly countered them with the usual reminders, 'It's such a small problem. I'll be away for only a few days . . .'. The effort paid off and the day began well. After dressing I stood gazing out at the noisy rain, seeing how the quiet-flowing river was being dimpled by the deluge. The long shower would help our vegetable seeds but I hoped the first tiny shoots wouldn't be crushed. We were already looking forward to a harvest of juicy young radishes before the month ended.

Friends from the city—Maureen and Peter—called in that morning, and it was a pleasure to sit down and talk over coffee. Good of them to drive all the way out from Aberdeen! I enjoyed their city news. It helped to stretch our minds further than village concerns. Maureen brought three packets of extra-special chocolate biscuits and I put them aside as a treat for Les and the boys during my absence. Before I had had time to refill the coffee cups Les and Peter had 'pushed open the hangar doors' and were enjoying a long discussion about their shared love—aircraft. It was good to see that once-familiar gleam come back into Les's eyes! Peter was doing some private flying out of Aberdeen in the hope of eventually obtaining a more permanent position, but competition was as keen as ever, while job opportunities continued to decrease.

'I feel for a young fellow starting out on a career in aviation now,' Les told me later. 'It's tough to be repeatedly rebuffed, specially after you've put so much effort and expense into training.'

While Les was thinking about Peter, my mind had gone back to something Maureen said: 'I feel Satan is really attacking you at present and I'm praying for the Lord to give you his victory'.

I hadn't really thought of my circumstances in terms of a direct satanic attack, yet surely that was a valid way in which to describe recent events? Didn't this make it all the more important for me to resist and fight? Yet at the same time I needed to hold firmly to the fact that Jesus was still stronger than even the most fierce onslaught. If I kept closely to him surely I must eventually win through?

By afternoon the rain had eased so Les put on old boots and went out to prepare the new side garden for bedding plants. He knew I wanted to buy some seedlings before going into hospital, so they would be flowering soon after my return.

'The new Ena Harkness climbing rose is already in bud!' Les reported happily when he came in for his mid-afternoon mug of tea.

By that time the kitchen was in a complete muddle because I was trying to make several batches of cakes and biscuits with which to fill the larder tins. There was milk spilled across the floor too because, in my haste, I'd tripped over Miss Puss's afternoon drink. One of the chocolate sponges was for Phyllis, who lived round the corner. I took it to her at teatime, wondering how she was coping with two new foster children as well as her own largish family.

'Oh, we're doing just fine!' Phyllis told me with a quick chuckle, when I handed over the cake (it looked rather small for so many hungry mouths), and I couldn't help admiring her cheerfulness, especially at the end of a long demanding day.

Clear sunlight suddenly burst out across the rain-washed sky that evening, so I took some sewing out onto the back doorstep and revelled in the clean fresh smell of the garden. Despite the earlier deluge, the seedling vegetables were reaching bravely up towards the golden sunshine, and away on the upstream bank of the river I noticed a purple lilac tree, just in bloom.

'Busy?' Les asked, coming out to sit beside me.

'Yes. Like it?'

I was turning up the hem of a new peach-coloured skirt which Rachel had made for me. It was a perfect fit and I was looking forward to wearing it with a matching blouse. How useful to have an eager-to-sew daughter!

Rachel would be arriving home next day, I remembered, and was sure to be full of her usual chatter about

the week's happenings in the radiography department.
She viewed the hospital in a completely different way, as
a source of interest and challenge, even pleasure at
times, and I always found it refreshing to listen and
enter into her eager, outgoing approach. Doing so helped
to offset my own anxiety. Another thought began to
interest me too, as I sat there on the garden step. Who
else would be in the ward with me this time? Were one
or two other housewives making themselves extra busy
at home this week in order to keep hospital apprehension
at bay? It was an intriguing, rather exciting thought to
realize we would soon be meeting up.

Every detail of the next hospital visit—even the new
friends I would make—was already known to God. The
thought comforted me, and I relaxed still more. Later,
when evening mist crept in across the river, we went
indoors and played a few rounds of a word game. Les
and Murray beat me hollow.

'And you're usually the expert!' Les teased. He'd scored
112 to my paltry forty-five. Murray made it to seventy-
eight. 'Must be losing my way with words,' I mumbled,
in mock despair.

*   *   *

Two days before Les's new work started we drove to
nearby Inverurie and bought a few dozen bedding plants,
mostly asters and my favourite stocks. Then, in the gleaming afternoon sunshine, Les planted out the seedlings
while all the blackbirds over in the far woods chorused
at full strength. A marvellous echo through the beech
trees! I sat on the garden seat and read through part of
the Old Testament book of Nehemiah, glad to be able to
concentrate more on reading. It had not been easy recently. Nehemiah had kept saying, 'The good hand of
my God was upon me,' and this repeated insistence,
amid extreme hardship, impressed me. But was God's
hand always good? And was his hand on me, too?

I began to understand that God *must* be good. Always
good. His complete goodness was part of what made

him God. There was evidence enough for his goodness in the intricate beauty and order of the world, as well as in the wonder of responding to his offered forgiveness in Jesus, so finding and delighting in him. To know and cherish God in your heart was to be finally convinced of his goodness.

Then too, God's good hand *was* on me because he'd particularly promised this to all who came to him. And even if such rich, completely undeserved goodness seemed too good to be true, there was more than enough evidence to show that it nonetheless was. Had I not already taken refuge in Jesus over and over again, finding him to be closer than anyone else could ever be, even Les? As I relaxed and gazed out across the river, trying to absorb all these different thoughts, words Anne had said, echoing Romans chapter 8, verse 28, came back to me: 'God does work everything together for good with those who love him, even if the events themselves can't be called good.'

Could I genuinely believe and rest back in that certainty? Sitting there in the garden I could. It was easy in the calm stillness at home. What about the following week? What about on Thursday, just before the operation? Would I be able to rest in God's utter goodness then? I wanted to know I would, but at such times I was so vulnerable, so easily frightened. For me those last moments as the anaesthetic took effect were worst of all, full of a terrible dark foreboding. In the quiet, flower-scented loveliness of that summer's afternoon I found myself reaching out again to God.

'Lord, keep your hand on me through all the experiences ahead. Please give me times of inner restfulness, just as you did before. I can't achieve such a rest on my own. I'm too quickly swamped by all the outer influences with which I'm surrounded.'

A friend's young daughter, Kate, was baptized at the Sunday service next day and, standing there by the font, our minister quoted Jesus' words, 'Except you become as a little child you shall not enter the kingdom ...' (Mt 18:2).

'What is the special characteristic of a little child?' Ian asked in his sermon later. 'A child is completely open, completely receptive . . .'

His words helped me, emphasizing my own need to be as trusting and receptive as a little child. Oh, but that was so hard! Trustfulness was natural to little children, automatically aware of their dependence, but it went against the grain for a complicated, independent adult. Did such a trust—such a faith—have to come completely as a gift from God? Did it have to be all of him from start to finish? Such a possibility was both humiliating and wonderful. Humiliating because I wanted to have at least one thing, even a faltering thing like my own trust, to offer him. Wonderful because, if it must be entirely of his giving, it would be like all his gifts, full of exciting potential, not at all weak and frail. I turned the thought over and over in my mind as we walked home from church, intrigued by this completely different angle on the matter. And I knew, as I considered it further, that this concept was not a mere 'possibility' at all. It was a basic truth, yet I had only just begun to glimpse it.

*   *   *

We had reached the last day of Les's short holiday. That evening he carefully laid out his clothes (including the new stiff-collared shirt) for work next morning and, watching, I felt so full of gladness for him. The next day must have seemed much like any other Monday for our neighbours along the street, but in our household it was definitely a red-letter occasion, and I took particular pleasure in kissing Les goodbye that morning. It had been so long since I'd kissed him on his way off to a *real* job. Then, standing on the wooden doorstep in the fresh glistening sunlight, I waved until the car turned the corner. The big day had come at last!

Within an hour Stuart burst in at the front door, just back from a week-long school trip to Shetland, and for the rest of the day kept rattling off details about 'a horizontal mill', 'a Bronze Age settlement', '*millions of* seals' and, 'Oh, you should have seen Fairisle, Mum! We went right past it in the ship last night. Great!' The two overnight ferry crossings had apparently been unusually calm by North Sea standards, and the days in between crammed full of worthwhile activity. 'The whole trip was fantastic, Mum! You'll just *have* to go there too!'

All through the day I tried to picture Les at work—meeting his four new colleagues, being briefed by the boss, seeing around the well-equipped control room. I also imagined him enjoying a delicious lunch in the company's cafeteria and guessed he'd choose a large exotic ice cream as dessert. The boys and I could hardly wait to bombard him with questions. Just after six o'clock that evening Stuart whooped, 'Here's Dad!' and rushed out to the door.

'How did the day go?'

'Have they given you lots of fancy computers to mess around with?'

'Did you get lost in all those corridors?'

'What was on the lunch menu?'

'Were they nice to you?'

Les could hardly get in through the door to give me his homecoming hug. The day had gone well. Les enjoyed meeting his boss and colleagues and was most impressed with the gas-flow control room.

'I'm going to have fun with those complex machines!' he told us, eyes shining. 'Things have certainly changed since I sent telex messages in the RAF thirty years ago!'

At last the lads let Les sit down at the supper table, but he hardly had room for the savoury pancakes I'd carefully prepared. 'My ice cream sundae at lunchtime was *huge*!' he told me, leaning back in the chair to rub his stomach. 'Peach-flavoured too!'

With the excitement of Les's work and Stuart's return from Shetland I had been happily distracted from thinking about the hospital admission, two days away. At odd moments through the day I'd completed the washing and ironing, and made out a long list of fresh food items to buy and store in the fridge next morning. Then there was some urgent mending to be done, and various phone calls to be made as well. 'I'm sure to forget something vital despite all my lists,' I kept worrying.

Anne had called in briefly during the afternoon and it had been good to sit down to talk and pray with her. As we chatted I sensed Anne's love and concern and this comforted me.

'One seemingly small thing is much on my mind,' I admitted, hesitantly. 'Could you help me with it in prayer?'

'Yes, of course. What is it?'

I explained my apprehension about the anaesthetic, the frightening foreboding when I was about to go under. Anne understood.

'I'm glad you told me,' she responded. 'Now I can specifically remember that in prayer. It helps to know actual fears, so I can really share them—and maybe take the load off you a little.'

5

'There Is a Way through This!'

Early next morning the thought of leaving the family filled me with sudden, sharp sadness, but after busying myself around the house I felt better, realizing again how good it had been of Jesus to give us the gladness of Les's starting work to make a sad week happier. Extra happy!

During the morning I cycled to the village shops and filled both bicycle baskets with groceries, topping the pile with a box of five seedling pansies for the front door trough. Then, back at the house, I planted them out as a way of expressing my confidence in soon being home to enjoy their colourful show. Some of the plants were already in bud.

Suzanne, a recently-met friend, came to my mind later so, after lunch, I set off to spend a while with her. As soon as we sat down she poured out the whole sad story of her marriage and the more I listened the more I felt for her. There could be no easy escape from so tight a tangle of personal circumstances and it was hard to know how to help, except by being an 'ear' and also encouraging Suzanne to seek expert advice. She'd already considered making an appointment, so I urged her to do so before the week was out.

As we talked young Jenny skipped in with a posy of small white daisies picked from the lawn for her mother. Suzanne forced a quick smile and laid the limp flowers down on the tile-topped coffee table. Somehow the never-

to-be-restored beauty of those frail daisies accentuated
the hopelessness deep in Suzanne's own heart and mind.
I thought of the huge problems those around us faced
every day while we knew nothing of them, only seeing a
row of colourful front doors set along a familiar street.
The lonely anguish was so carefully shut away.

When I reached home I took out the small blue suitcase
and began to put back several of the items I'd so eagerly
unpacked a few weeks earlier. There was also the expensive lavender soap a neighbour, Kate, had thoughtfully given, and a bottle of eau de cologne sent by Lin, a
friend who lived just outside the village. I knew I would
particularly value those touches of love and concern this
time, but didn't need to pack much else. The case felt
quite light when I picked it up, and the contents tumbled
together. 'I'll soon be home!' I remembered happily.
Would the mauve and pink stocks be flowering then?
Would there be a red velvet bloom on the Ena Harkness
rose?

Late at night as I lay in bed (pretending to be asleep so
that Les would relax and go to sleep too), I deliberately
made myself think ahead. After all, there was the whole
summer to anticipate!

'You'll be able to lie out on the lawn and get fat and
sunburnt!' friends had been encouraging me and their
words kept coming back into my mind. Then there was
the twins' sixteenth birthday to anticipate too, just a
week away. I was sure to be home and able to join in the
celebrations by then. In fact, I had deliberately not baked
a cake in advance because it would be much more fun
for Les to choose a delicious gateau on the day he drove
me home. Then we could make it a double celebration!

My thoughts were strangely eager and excited, full of
plans. Not at all gloomy or self-pitying. Why did I feel so
unexpectedly positive? Was it because my mind, baulking
at continued apprehension, had suddenly swung right
over to the opposite extreme by way of escape? Then
too, I'd reached that welcome threshold when all the
happenings I'd dreaded were about to take place, to
move from the future to the past, so setting me free. I

wouldn't need to be trapped by fear or anticipation any more. It would all be over.

But could I ever be really free of fear now? Wouldn't I always wonder about a recurrence? No, on this particular night I was not even going to contemplate such a possibility. I only wanted to get beyond the small operation and come home to the family, the garden, and the loveliness of an unfolding summer. Everything else must be shut out of my mind. I wanted to dismiss and forget it, to live as if it could never happen.

I gazed out of the window as midnight approached. The sky was washed with deep purple, empty of clouds, and I could see the last few rooks beating their way slowly over towards the far hills. The scent of wild flowers, strong and sweet, drifted in through the open window and I could even smell the fresh, foaming cleanness of the murmuring Don. Everything seemed more vivid than ever before, poignant, suddenly valuable. I began to store each memory carefully in my mind so that I could relive it over and over again in the few days ahead.

*   *   *

'Bye Mum! Hope it goes all right for you!' Stuart yelled, before running for his bus early next morning.

'Goodbye then,' Murray murmured as he wandered out of the back door, almost late for school.

'Come and see me, won't you?' I called after him. Les washed the few breakfast dishes while I fussed over my hair and collected my raincoat. 'Have I remembered everything?' I wondered, lingering in the warmth and homeliness of our livingroom. Miss Puss sniffed her way around the blue suitcase but didn't even twitch a whisker when I stroked her goodbye. 'Come on!' Les said, putting his hand on my shoulder. 'Time to be off!'

Eager for the day to be as ordinary as possible, I'd planned for Les to drive me across the hill to our minister's house, before going on to work. Mary would then take me to the main hospital entrance, on the way to her own department. It was grey and drizzly as we climbed into the car and the new seedlings in the side border were dripping with rain. I couldn't resist a quick glance back at the house and garden as Les pulled away from the kerb.

'This time next week I'll be home again!' I reminded him. He reached out to squeeze my knee.

'Yes, and then we'll celebrate!'

The village seemed strangely unfamiliar at such an early hour of the day and I looked around, fascinated. There were so many cars, so many scampering school-children along the usually quiet side-streets. We passed Marion, waiting at a side junction, and she waved and smiled. Then we passed the crowded Aberdeen-bound bus down near the pleasure park, picking up still more passengers. Les left me in Mary's warm kitchen.

'Bye! I'll come and see you tonight!'

Mary and I chatted all the way to the city and I enjoyed pretending it was just an ordinary trip for shopping or a picnic by the sea. Everyone in her family was busy plan-ning for an approaching wedding and it was fun to discuss different costume ideas. Then, as we neared the hospital, I caught sight of a familiar figure at the kerbside. It was one of the friends I had met in the ward last time. How well she looked now! I watched her hurry across the road to the shop where she worked and suddenly longed to be starting an ordinary, predictable day too, just as she was. What would my friend have said if she'd known I was passing on my way back to the ward? For those few moments, as I watched her, recent events seemed so unlikely, so unbelievable. Had it all really happened?

By now Mary was slowing the car down, ready to turn in at the hospital gate. She pulled up near the main door and helped me out with the case.

'We'll be thinking of you,' she said gently.

'Thank you. I do value that so much!'

Inside the stiff double doors the air was hot and heavy with the mingled smells of rubber-tiled floors and anti-septic. The wide hall was still almost empty, the bank and shop closed. One or two other new patients were sitting at the far end, tense and hypersensitive to every surrounding sight and sound. I walked on past them and found the small cafeteria just open, so bought a beaker of tea and sat down at the window table where we had met up with Rachel just a week or two before. The wet mist was curling around the grey granite buildings, and gulls were flocked on the green lawns beyond, motionless in the cold rain. Half a dozen ward orderlies arrived, chatting and laughing as they sank into the cafeteria chairs, then opened thermos flasks and spread out their morning newspapers. How I enjoyed their loud cheerfulness! For a few moments I glimpsed their ordinary, unremarkable day and felt almost included.

When nine o'clock came I stood up, threw the disposable beaker into a nearby waste bin, and went to the registration desk to hand over the admission letter. The formalities were straightforward—'That's fine, Mrs Brown, just take the lift to the second floor, then turn right into the ward!'—but intensely hard. I wanted to rush back through the stiff main doors and out along the crowded city streets to the quiet countryside. Oh, if only I could have gone back to an easy, routine, secure day! But it was foolish to think like that, so I made myself smile, and nodded in response to the receptionist, then walked briskly to the lift, determined to look calm and confident. No one must know about the inner fear. I was not even going to confess it to myself.

Beyond the ward door I caught sight of Mary, the African student nurse who had been such a friend before. 'What are *you* doing here?' she called out, smiling in greeting, and hurrying to take my case.

'Oh, just calling in for a day or two. Nothing much,' I told her, as she took my arm and led me to the admission room. It meant so much to be welcomed by Mary, and I sensed Jesus had planned that small, significant touch because he knew I was inwardly very anxious. I could not hide my fear from him. While checking me in Mary said, 'It's good we met today because tomorrow I'm leaving for another ward, and then we'd have missed each other!'

Another nurse led me to a four-bedded room and the three other patients, all older, looked up and smiled when I joined them, then went on reading their newspapers. I remembered the card Kate had slipped through the letterbox just before I left home so, after unpacking, sat self-consciously on the edge of the bed and opened it up—a watercolour of a summer cornfield with birds and wild flowers in the foreground. It was so fresh and full of life and I studied the card for a long time, taking in each detail. Kate little knew how much the painting meant to me that difficult morning.

And so the long day passed, full of varied happenings. A liver scan was done and, 'Guess what, the result is normal!' Mary, the house-surgeon, told me later, when she came into the ward to greet me.

'Then surely you won't have to operate!' I cried, full of instant excitement. I could go home after all! I could forget about the hospital, the problem, the fear! . . .

'No, I'm afraid the operation is still on,' Mary said slowly. 'The ultrasound would have been unlikely to show so small an area of involvement, so we were expecting a normal result.'

She sat down on the bed and I valued a chance to talk. 'I was quite shocked when I saw the path. report,' Mary went on. 'But then I thought how good it was that the problem had been discovered at such an early stage, when it could be easily treated. If the other operation hadn't been done we'd never have found this small growth. It would have gone on slowly enlarging until it became very invasive and impossible to remove. So we can be glad after all about the way everything has worked out! I'm sure God's wise hand has been in it all.'

Mary was right. This was turning out for good in my life even though, for the moment, I resented the problem so much. That was because I could only see it from a limited short-term viewpoint. God saw the matter from beginning to end, in its completeness, and surely what he was allowing now was important to that final enriching completeness? Couldn't I open myself to this and so relax?

I was still thinking about Mary's words when the lunch trays came round. Then Sheila called in unexpectedly (good to see a familiar face from the village!) bringing me a thick, glossy magazine. A real treat! Maureen came during the afternoon visiting hours showing particular concern.

'We're all praying for you,' she said, and by 'all' I knew she meant friends at her church whom I'd never even met. What a humbling realization! Les came at tea-time, on his way home from work, and we talked superficially about the day's happenings because neither of us could put deeper thoughts into words. Everything had gone well at work and he'd been asked to attend a one-day telex course at the central post office the following Monday.

'You'll have a whale of a time there!' I teased and then, together, we walked down the corridor to the day room.

'See over there, on the flat roof?' I said, pointing out of the window.

'See what?'

'That small round scraping of stones, and the two nestlings close by.'

'Oh . . . yes!' and Les bent closer to the glass. 'Oyster-catchers!'

Earlier in the day the friendly ward orderly had pointed out the parent birds to me, then the two chicks resting in the shadow of the roof parapet, thin legs stretched straight out behind their down-covered bodies. Such fun to watch! Les was fascinated too. 'We must show them to Murray when he comes in!'

My last visitor of the day was Mr H. who tiptoed into the ward. 'Do you mind if I visit?'

I was so glad to see him, and we talked together for a while before he prayed with me. Simple, direct words, asking Jesus to keep me through the operation next day, and to bring a good outcome from it. It was particularly helpful to hear someone else finding clear, audible words for my own hard-to-express requests, and I longed to say an adequate 'thank you' to him, but the words wouldn't come.

At last the evening sunlight began to fade and the night staff drew the blinds, shutting out the bustling life and lights of the city. Then, when they had given us sleeping tablets, everything became quiet. There was nothing now to distract me from thinking about the next day. But hadn't Mr H. committed it all to God? And hadn't I added my own 'amen'? Was I now going to allow fear to swamp me again? I could feel it thrusting back. Fear about going under the anaesthetic, fear about the actual operation, fear about the risk of a later recurrence of the illness. It was the same old onslaught, more insistent still because it had been firmly kept in check all day. I was too tired to resist. My defences were right down.

'Lord Jesus, I admit I'm afraid,' I cried inwardly. 'All that previous fear is moving back in and I've no strength left to tackle it. I'm too weak. Please help me fight it.'

I could feel the sedative taking effect. My thinking was becoming blurred, disconnected. I longed to lie back against Jesus, to rest in his protection, knowing the strong safety of such a refuge. 'Dear Lord, please keep me, whatever lies ahead.'

*   *   *

The following morning—foodless and drinkless—seemed extra long. When the newspapers came round I remembered it was general election day. People would already be voting, all agog with excited suspense. But no one mentioned the election there in the ward. They didn't even switch on the television. I tried reading the glossy magazine, then writing a thank you note to Kate, then knitting a complicated jersey pattern, but when I looked at my watch it was still only 9.30 a.m. So then I tried chatting in the day room, or strolling down the corridor, or watching the young oyster-catchers scampering across their flat roof home.

'There are only two operations this afternoon,' one of the other patients announced later, across the day room lunch table. 'One's big and one's very small. I overheard the doctors saying so.'

'Mine's the very small one,' I commented, reassured to be placed in so simple a category. Soon afterwards the staff nurse called me for the pre-operative injection and almost immediately drowsiness began to cloud my thinking. But not for long. 'Maybe I won't be home for the twins' birthday after all,' I thought all of a sudden. 'Maybe I should have ordered a special cake?' The concern nagged at my mind, becoming more insistent. Would Anne be able to help? I must phone her. There was still time. I got up and walked dazedly down the corridor to the phone trolley, hoping the staff nurse was away at lunch. Anne sounded surprised to hear my voice, but was more than willing to take care of the birthday cake order.

'I'll place it at the post office shop tomorrow,' she promised. 'Now go back and lie down before you get caught . . . and don't forget I'll be praying specially for you when they give you that anaesthetic injection in an hour or so.'

It had helped to talk to Anne and I appreciated being able to draw again on the comfort of her friendship. It was easier to rest now and, lying down, I began to think of the many different people who had promised to pray —Helen, Thea, Hazel, Mary and Ian, Maureen and Peter, different family members, and many more friends down south. I pictured them in their different homes, 'visiting' with them in my mind until the drowsiness increased. I was certainly not alone. They were all with me!

The theatre lad came, and began skilfully manoeuvering my bed. 'Lord, keep me now. Go with me . . .' I was very sleepy. The day room ladies stood up and called, 'You'll be back very soon!' The theatre porter chatted to his mate in the lift. 'It was a great game last night, wasn't it! Full of fast action!' The doors of the theatre wing swung open as we approached. There were glaring lights straight above and the warm air was full of that sickly-sweetness of anaesthetics. I lay very still, trying hard to

be open to Jesus' reassurance so that I would not feel too
afraid. All around I could hear voices, echoes, laughing,
the click of instruments, the faint hum of machinery,
but everything seemed distant and indistinct.

'You're from Donside?' a young nurse beside me asked.
'Nice up there, isn't it? I've an aunt at Monymusk.'

Someone came up close to the trolley and bent down.
It was Mary, the house-surgeon, though for a moment I
didn't recognize her in theatre clothing. How much it
meant to see a friendly face, and to feel Mary's hand.
She had sensed my fear.

'You'll be all right!' Mary whispered. 'It will soon be
over.' And I remembered Anne's promise of prayer. A
doctor connected up some tubing, inserted an intravenous needle, and started to give the anaesthetic. Instantly I felt myself going, falling faster and faster, further and further into the strange cold darkness.

*   *   *

Much later I vaguely saw Les. Maybe the kindly surgeon
was there too? Then everything became dark. The following hours were indistinct. Sometime during the night I
woke, feeling an intense pain in my right side. It was
difficult to breathe. I lay there for a while, not wanting
to disturb the other patients, but the pain kept increasing.
Dr Mary passed in the corridor and saw I was awake, so
tiptoed in.

'Wait, I'll bring you an injection for the pain,' she
promised, and I was soon able to relax and breathe
more easily.

'That's a great relief,' I whispered to Mary. 'I'm so
grateful.' I was grateful not to have an intravenous drip
this time, too, and this seemed to confirm that it had
been a very small operation, just as the surgeon had
expected. 'I'll soon be better . . . I'll soon be home . . .' I
thought happily as the drowsiness returned.

I dozed during the day, though was often disturbed
by sudden frightening dreams, as if a dark, sinister
power was clutching at me, determined to take me into

its grip. It was impossible adequately to describe the feeling, though I guessed it could be a side-effect of the strong painkilling injections. Did habitual drugtakers, for all their eagerly sought 'highs' also experience a similar terrifying darkness, I wondered, and shuddered for them. Once or twice, feeling desperate, I simply cried 'Jesus!' (silently, in my heart) and relief came. How much this meant, especially as it so graphically confirmed Jesus' greater power over dark forces.

Les called in after work but I couldn't keep my eyes open for long. Rachel came several times, spending her coffee and tea breaks with me, as well as most of her lunch hour. Before leaving in the evening she brushed my hair and helped me with a mouthwash. It greatly refreshed me and I appreciated being ministered to in these basic ways by my own daughter. We were being drawn closer still to one another. The surgeon came round soon after Rachel left.

'Tomorrow I'll start you on a special drink in order to try to avoid intravenous fluids,' he told me, then noticing my pain, asked the staff nurse to give me another injection. I welcomed the gradual relief it gave, though felt apprehensive about further frightening dreams. But maybe I would sleep too deeply to dream this time? My mind was tired. Too tired to think of Jesus being with me. But he *was* still with me, even within me, feeling my pain. How tender and complete was his identification.

The strange blurred day ended as the hot golden sun burned low on the rooftop horizon, and I could hear the parent oyster-catchers screaming, each cry answered by an eerie echo. The long night's silence had begun.

When the day staff swarmed in early next morning I asked who had won the election.

'Maggie again!' one of the student nurses announced, 'So some people will be glad, I suppose.'

She picked up my glossy magazine and began searching for tips on cookery and furnishings. 'Must get all clued-up before my wedding in September!' she explained, then showed me the diamond cluster ring kept carefully pinned inside her pocket. It was fun to chat about her plans and ideas.

'Now, look at that exotic bathroom suite! Fancy a fuschia-coloured oval-shaped split-level bath?' she giggled. 'Oh, and here's a lacy-draped four-poster. Can't see my guy lying down under all that!'

The ward sister marched past, checking up on her staff. 'Hey, I'm supposed to be getting you lot out of bed!' The young nurse leapt to attention and, because I was nearest, started on me. The pain and effort of getting up was well worthwhile and I felt proud of my progress as I sat by the window, looking at the many cards and notes friends had sent. Heavy footsteps in the corridor outside meant ward rounds were starting, and when the surgeon reached our room he came straight over to where I was sitting. 'We'll soon have you right again!' he promised, pausing to prescribe the special drinks, then he bent to give me a quick pat on the shoulder. 'You're getting on like a house on fire!'

I was grateful for his encouragement. It kept going through my mind. 'I could even be home tomorrow!' I thought. 'That would be on my fourth day, just as he said.' Half an hour passed. A strange dizziness began, so a couple of nurses put me back to bed, and I felt grateful for their concern. What a difference it made to be constantly helped and cared for when you weren't feeling too well, and yet so many people, some perhaps only a short distance from the hospital, were facing various kinds of suffering alone and uncared for. 'How hard that must be,' I realized as I lay back and looked out across the rows and rows of city homes. Would I feel more keenly for such people in future? Would I give myself to helping ease their pain?

As the day wore on I felt shivery and unwell. It hadn't been like that after the previous surgery. By the second day I had already started to bounce back, and this time it had only been so small an operation. Surely I should be making even faster progress? The contrast troubled me. I lay looking out through the slats of the blinds, seeing how the heat haze trembled in the still, suffocating air. It was a scorching day and I guessed the beach boulevard would be busy. Quite a rare occurrence in the north, even on summer weekends. When Les and the boys visited in the afternoon I urged them to go to the sea front afterwards. 'It will be marvellous down there today!'

'Yes, I guess it will. Perhaps we'll do that,' Les agreed.

Later, after the family had gone and the room was suddenly silent, I missed all the eager chatter about Stuart's 'kartie' and Murray's yacht. My mind pictured the three of them at the beach, then driving home and sitting around the supper table, full of the usual teasing and arguing. I missed not being a part of it, not being able to draw on Les's companionship and the reassurance of talking at length together. Most of all I missed not caring for the family, choosing the lads' favourite menus or shopping for small extras for Rachel's larder. (She was trying to survive on a shoestring and I doubted if she fed herself adequately.) I missed the ordinariness of home, its security and relaxation. There in the hospital people were either withdrawn and anxious, or else talkative about their illnesses. Everyone was watching everyone else, observing treatments, predicting outcomes. Illness was the common bond, the first thought on waking and the last on drifting back to sleep. Everything revolved around its reality. An anxious, unnatural world, irksome in the extreme. How I longed to be free, to go home and leave it all finally behind.

Around 6 p.m., while I was deep in thought, our Aberdeen friends, Win and Priscilla, arrived. It was Win's weekend off from busy work in the hospital, yet he still came to visit. We talked for a while and I admired Priscilla's smart dress. 'It's Sunday, of course, and they're on their way to church,' I thought. Time was going by.

'Don't stay any longer,' I told them. 'You'll be late for the evening service.'

But they just smiled. 'We've plenty of time.' Several more minutes passed.

'You must go now!' I insisted, anxious not to keep them from church.

'No, it's all right. We've come to see *you* this evening,' Priscilla explained.

After a while another city friend, Margaret, arrived, carrying a large and very lovely bouquet of yellow crysanthemums, red carnations and orange tiger lilies. So colourful!

'We'll go now,' Win said, and they slipped away. It was good to talk to Margaret for a while and then, when she had gone, I lay back wondering how late Win and Priscilla had been for church. Suddenly I realized, 'It isn't Sunday, it's only Saturday!' I could feel my face flushing with embarrassment. What must they have thought? Did they wonder if I was becoming disorientated? Yet they couldn't have been more reassuring, wanting to spare me. I felt foolish and upset because I had never made a mistake like that, being proud of my clear, ordered mind. Was this confusion due to the anaesthetic and other drugs? Or to the increasing tension with which I was struggling?

Last thing that night I took a 'sip' from the small New Testament I'd brought with me. 'He [Jesus] said to me "My grace is sufficient for you, for my power is made perfect in weakness." I will all the more gladly boast of my weaknesses, that the power of Christ may rest upon me' (2 Cor 12:9).

I remembered how I'd always boasted inwardly of my efficiencies, despising weakness. (How I despised my present physical weakness and dull mind!) Yet wasn't it also important to boast of my dependency, simply because it accentuated my need of Jesus, and so compelled me to respond to him the more? I began to realize that these two—the pride of independence and the pride of dependence—were not intended to conflict. Independence was part of my rightful human dignity, put there by God, and important to coping with life. But it was essential that there be a point at which, aware also of human frailty, I admitted my great need of Christ and allowed him to take over. So couldn't I boast of my limiting weakness if, because of it, I came to possess Jesus' richness in the Holy Spirit—Jesus himself—more and more? Compared to so great a possession human independence seemed a small thing indeed. My mind was tired but I was nonetheless intrigued by this truth and its meaning, feeling a need to explore it further. Maybe later on, when my thinking was more sharp and clear?

*   *   *

The unaccustomed heatwave continued and next day the ward grew hotter still as shafts of strong sunlight thrust in through the half-open blinds. It seemed strange that it should be Sunday, for the day was much like any other, except that the ward was very quiet. I planned to go to the chapel service downstairs, but when the pain in my side unexpectedly increased, the ward sister insisted I needed rest. The problem soon eased, without an injection. I was definitely progressing, even in so small a way, and was also doing well on sips of the peculiar green liquid the surgeon recommended. It tasted of sweet-salty lemon juice.

After visiting hours, Les took the lads on to tea with Maureen and Peter. It was generous of them to invite our hungry fellows over when they already had a large family to feed themselves. Things seemed to be going smoothly at home and Les was careful to tell me he'd remembered to buy extra milk and bread for the weekend.

'You see, we can manage without you!' he insisted, squeezing my hand. But deep down I didn't really want them to manage for long. I wanted to be needed by them all again.

All day I felt low—physically, mentally, spiritually—though it hurt my pride to admit it. I struggled to keep bright and optimistic on the outside and hoped the cover-up convinced others, but inwardly I was very dull, despondent too at times. It was proving much harder to keep positive this time, perhaps because I was more weak and ill physically, and yet I still hoped to be home at least on my fifth day, though the surgeon had made no mention of the possibility. Was he going to keep me in hospital until my temperature settled? Until the re-

curring pain had gone? Until I could eat again? But how
long would that take? Somehow I couldn't relax and be
at peace, nor could I even think of boasting about my
weakness. I resented weakness intensely, longing only to
be normal and well and strong again—soon. Then I
would be able to forget myself, finding release from
irksome self-preoccupation.

I was also aware of a growing inner sadness, mingled
with the recurrent fear. Though hard to define, it was
sometimes disturbingly real. I longed somehow to express it and perhaps find an escape through crying, yet
held back from doing so. Tears would give the lie to my
careful cover-up, and once I started crying it might be
hard to stop. 'No, I must not let myself cry,' I resolved,
'but maybe I could talk to someone and so begin to
understand my sadness better by putting it all into
words?'

I realized the 'someone' would need to be outside my
situation in order to be entirely objective and in no way
disturbed. I missed Mary, the student nurse, who had
been such a friend. Though young and comparatively
carefree, she had nonetheless shown a remarkable degree of perception and concern. This awareness on her
part would have made it possible for me to talk to her
about my feelings and even, perhaps, to find relief in
tears. But Mary had gone, of course, and I knew the
doctors on our ward were far too busy for a long, somewhat complex off-loading. How about the rest of the
nursing staff? Somehow, for all their kindness, they
seemed strangely unapproachable. Their work was done
carefully and well; they anticipated and met require-
ments, but everything was kept very much to a practical
level. The day-to-day programme didn't allow a slot for
sitting and talking about deeper needs, so any such
availability would have had to be an extra, and far from
easy at that.

My mind went back to my own nursing training. 'Never
get emotionally involved with patients,' we were, quite
rightly, cautioned. Such a degree of involvement would
soon have swamped us, escape becoming impossible even

during off-duty hours. So, playing safe, we usually veered to the other extreme, limiting care to the strictly practical too. It was familiar ground where we could operate with confidence. But sit and listen as a patient wept out his long sorrow? No. At least, only on very rare occasions, and even then we would hardly have known how to respond. Perhaps I had nursed many patients struggling with this same heavy sadness who, at crisis points longed to talk, yet were frustrated by the same lack of a caring, listening ear?

Was it possible for a nurse to become fully available without at the same time being emotionally swamped? In fact, how could any helping person achieve the needed balance? I sensed the secret lay in reaching out a strong, concerned hand—'I'm right here, available to you . . .'— while at the same time keeping one's own feet on firm, objective ground in order to have helpful resources, practical and advisory, upon which to draw. On the other hand, those who leapt into the problem with the sufferer not only became emotionally overwhelmed themselves, but were also left with nothing to offer.

I had never stopped to think all this through before, but my own inner longing for help that afternoon forced me to do so. It had been interesting to work out the most effective approach to a person's need too. Maybe this would prove important in future when I met others who felt a deep longing to talk about unexpressed sadness and fear? Meanwhile, feeling unable myself to confide in those around me, I decided to try and smother the sorrow. But, deep down, I knew this to be unwise. It would grow the more through such a dismissal.

*   *   *

Moving around was easier now so I decided to walk a short distance along the ward corridor by way of a distraction from inward thinking. The idea worked and I was more than pleased when the staff nurse passed and commented, 'You're getting on well!' I smiled. Yes, I would be back in action again soon. I must be!

That night I couldn't sleep even though the room was cool at last, and the dull ache in my side had been eased by tablets. In the shadowy semi-darkness, problems swelled to large, threatening proportions making dismissal almost impossible. During the day I had tried to keep anxiety at bay by deliberately participating in the ward routine but now there was no such distraction and it began to force itself into my mind, demanding attention. I wanted to escape into deep, protective sleep, but every time I tried to do so fear dragged me back, more insistent than ever.

One particularly disturbing fear returned now that I had emerged from the deadening influence of strong drugs, constantly confronting me with a single, stark fact: 'A liver malignancy is bad.' A neighbour had made that statement some years earlier, adding, 'If it gets to your liver, well, that's it!' How her words haunted me now. But I was determined not to entertain such a statement for long, countering it with a strong and immediate objection. 'This primary kind is different. It doesn't spread. It doesn't return.' Yet, even though I tried to insist on these facts I couldn't fully believe them, and fear immediately leapt back through the narrow chink of doubt to reassert itself. 'A liver malignancy is bad . . . .' 'No, no, not this kind!' And so the mind-battle intensified.

'Lord, please help me in my weakness,' I found myself pleading. 'I can't win on my own. Please bring this inner conflict to an end so I can sleep.'

This time, in the absence of distracting outward activity, I found I must discipline my mind to create its own diversion, centring it on the many good things I was experiencing in hospital: the surgeon's kindness, thoughtful nursing care, the companionship of other patients, the joy of visits, letters, cards, flowers. There *was* so much cause for gratitude! In time I felt a little more at ease, but it was impossible to relax completely. Eventually weariness clouded my thinking and I fell asleep around 3 a.m. just as the night staff were gathering in the nearby kitchen for morning tea.

Les came to my mind as soon as I woke. He'd be spending the day at the main post office, absorbing information about all those new, complex telex machines. As the morning passed I tried to picture him there, imagining his pleasure at such an opportunity. He'd already told me how touch-typing skills, learned years before during National Service, were now proving a considerable asset as he operated computer keyboards in the control room. So much was 'working together for good'!

'Les looks a completely different person!' friends had started to remark, and they were right. He did look different. The strain had faded from his face and a quiet confidence was gradually taking its place. It gave me joy to picture him as I sat there by the wide hospital window that morning.

All the while I was straining my ears for the surgeon's voice out in the corridor, and the sound of several approaching footsteps. (He was always accompanied by a few colleagues.) He was sure to talk about my going home. Maybe tomorrow?

It was almost coffee time before the surgeon came. He studied each chart, asked about the drinks, and suggested starting on a high-protein diet, then moved on to the next patient, but not before patting my shoulder and saying, 'Don't worry, you're heading in the right direction!'

A huge, unreasonable disappointment began to sweep right over me. It was a struggle to keep back the tears. How childish to weep just because I could not be home with Les and the boys. Determined to fight self-pity, I eased myself up from the bed and walked out into the corridor, catching sight of a new patient sitting alone in the day room. She was a slim, attractive young girl, struggling to hide her apprehension, just as I had done the first morning. I walked across and tried to put her at ease by pointing out the oyster-catcher chicks on the roof below. (They'd grown fast, even in four days!) Irene seemed to want to talk, even if falteringly, and I realized she was facing a large, frightening operation

with far-reaching consequences. Maybe she was fearing
a malignancy too? (I still refused the word 'cancer' in my
thinking), though she didn't refer directly to this. I could
understand her reticence. As we talked, part of my
anxiety about myself switched to Irene. I began to extend
my concern to her as well, feeling the acute inner hurt of
being crushed by circumstances. She became silent, unwilling to say more, so I sat with her for a while trying to
sort out the muddle I had made of my knitting the
previous week, just before the operation.

Later, during the usual after-lunch lull, I glanced
through an old nineteenth century edition of Frances
Ridley Havergal's book *Kept for the Master's Use*. Years
before Thea had picked it up from a book barrow in
Charing Cross Road and given it to me as a birthday
present, and I had been glad to have this favourite book
for company in hospital even though I hadn't actually
opened it until now. Flicking through its pages I remembered how Frances had learned the enrichment of
resting patiently back in God, despite prolonged physical
suffering. Yet this time, as I reread a few paragraphs
(my mind was too dull for more) I felt unable to apply
such a quiet, unquestioning trust to my own circumstances. It seemed unreasonable. I still wanted to fight
against weakness, rather than acquiesce, so put the book
back into the locker cupboard and lay quietly for a
while, looking at the flowers and cards on the windowsill,
then at the intensely blue sky beyond. A phrase from
Colossians (Col 1:11) crept into my mind. Perhaps I had
read it recently? 'Patience with joy'.

The 'with joy' emphasis was important. Not at all a
grudged patience, endured with long sighs, but something altogether different. A glad and creative patience,
which could eventually open a person's eyes to valuable
truths, well nigh impossible to recognize by any other
means. Oh, but such patience seemed so hard! It didn't
come easily to an active, restless, determined individual
like me. I wasn't even sure I wanted that kind of patience
yet. Fighting against circumstances seemed preferable,
more admirable too.

Someone tiptoed into the room at 3 p.m. It was Linda, a friend with whom I had recently corresponded. Lovely actually to see her! She stayed for over an hour and I valued her gift of time on a busy Monday. How much she encouraged me!

After Linda had gone I realized how important it was to visit and sit at leisure with people, listening and caring. I had always found it hard to give the gift of time, whether to family members or friends. My programme was deliberately crammed with planned activity, things done as, when, and how I wanted to do them. But, if I offered another person an hour or so of my day, I would have to forego this freedom for a little while. A small, worthwhile sacrifice, and yet extraordinarily difficult to consider. Why? I suppose it was because, until now, I had not stopped to think of the person on the receiving end of the gift, and of their need for an unhurried, listening ear. So many lonely, anxious people longed for such a gift, for it could make all the difference to a tedious, empty day. Was the foregoing of an hour's time really such a hardship when it could give another person such simple pleasure, and bring me, the time-giver, unexpected gladness too? Was it a practical, everyday example of 'patience with joy'?

Linda little knew how her visit had started off a whole new line of thinking, confronting me with a needed readjustment of priorities I could not ignore. Perhaps too, this discovery was yet another aspect of the learning experience God intended for me through my own time of difficulty?

When Les arrived some time later, with Stuart in tow, he was full of enthusiasm about the post office day course. 'You should have seen those machines. Quite something!' So I quizzed him for more details, just to share his excitement the more. Stuart lay across the bottom of the bed eating chocolates and all but one small bunch of grapes. He was in a jubilant mood too, after completing the next stage of his 'kartie' at school.

'You must see it Mum. Talk about being built for speed! Just you wait till I get it out on the back road!'

After supper the evening visiting hour brought four more friends, including Mr H. and, following introductions around the circle, we had a lively discussion on all kinds of topics, which was appreciated because then I could forget about hospitals, illnesses, and future prognoses. After they had gone I took stock of things and realized I was definitely much better. My mind was more clear too. No risk of mistaking Saturday for Sunday now. The dull ache was being well controlled by tablets and my raised temperature had begun to slide down. I was certain the surgeon would be pleased next day. Maybe I could start eating then too? And perhaps I'd be allowed home by Wednesday? In fact, I was determined to be home by then. Wednesday was the boys' birthday! Les had bought a spanner set for Stuart and a digital watch for Murray, and Anne would be collecting the cake sometime on Tuesday. Yes, the more I thought about it the more sure I was of being there to join in all the celebrations.

My confidence rose still further when, on getting up next morning, I found it easier still to move around. There wasn't even a slight tug from the stitches now. I walked down to the end of the corridor and watched the breeze tousling new leaves on a tree beside the main gate. The ward sister had been cosseting a tomato plant on the windowsill there and it was tall and healthy, laden with small green fruit. I caught sight of Irene, alone in her room watching breakfast television, so spent a short while with her, but she was much too upset to say more than a few words. Her operation was planned for a couple of hours later. I felt the more deeply for her as we sat together, and sensed something of the struggle in her mind, the anger which she couldn't put into words.

'Why should this have happened to me?'

'Why does a loving God allow such suffering?'

'Where is God in all of this anyway?'

I wanted to try to help Irene but realized that, as yet, I had no clearly thought out response to such questioning and despair. It wouldn't have been appropriate to intrude into her deliberately chosen silence either. She wanted to be alone with her thoughts, however distressing.

Despite the occasion two days earlier when I had so much wanted to talk to someone, I still clung to silence most of the time. A person generally chose to battle alone, the yearning for a listening partner being rare, but nonetheless distressingly insistent when it came. Such contrasting attitudes had always puzzled me, but I was beginning to understand them now. If a friend probed when you preferred silence you struggled the more to hide or deny the pain, and it was important for the probing person to be sensitive to this and stop.

If, on the other hand, someone shrugged you off when you longed to share, the inner pressure was likely to increase to an unbearable pitch and you would need to obtain relief somehow, eventually seeking it in weeping or by some form of expressed anger, if by no other way. This probably explained any unpredictable or irrational behaviour on the part of a person struggling with inner distress, and whereas I had once considered it best merely to soothe and then forget such an outburst, I now realized it was much more helpful if friends or family could take time and effort to understand by asking a leading question (which would release the torrent of anguish if the time was right), or by simply sitting and keeping a distressed person company, feeling *with* them rather than merely for them, until the inner pain eased.

Had it helped Irene to have someone sit with her? I didn't know, but after a while she turned to give me a quick, hesitant smile. 'It'll soon be over,' she said. The staff nurse came in with Irene's pre-operative injection so I stood up and left quietly, my heart heavy for her. But surely Jesus would go with her into the experience ahead? Surely she would feel him to be there?

*   *   *

Later that morning a student dietician came to discuss menu ideas with me. She also promised to make up frequent high-protein drinks 'to help put back some

weight'. I was glad to hear her mention this for my
thinness was making me feel all the more self-conscious.
At least it didn't show too much under a long flowing
housecoat, but what about when I tried wearing daytime
outfits at home? At lunchtime the nurses brought me
the first drink, made from eggs, milk, orange juice and
high calorie sugar. It tasted extra-delicious and I hoped
the young dietician would return so I could mention
how much her efforts were being appreciated.

After sipping the drink—it was marvellously cool!— I
took Frances Ridley Havergal's book out of the locker
cupboard again and this time tried to consider her quiet
trustfulness as being more appropriate than a violent
reaction against circumstances. Her attitude also matched
the Corinthian verse about experiencing Jesus' all-important inner strength only as a result of first acknow-
ledging (even boasting about) personal weakness. Surely
this acknowledgement and its resultant rest were essential before I could take hold of the inward power and
mastery I needed so much? Mary Craig had written
words which fitted well: '. . . there is a way through this,
but you must find it outside of yourself. Remember I am
here, in the darkness. You are never alone.'*

Wasn't this what Jesus had wanted me to understand
and grasp all those long weeks ago, that only after quiet,
deliberate relinquishment and resting back would I be
in a position to take hold of what he waited to give me?
But I had been too busy trying to fight circumstances in
my own dwindling strength, all the while becoming more
and more frustrated.

In fact, even the relinquishment and rest had to be his
gift, achieved only as I let him achieve it for me, and the
outcome would be acceptance of present circumstances,
rather than a constant chafing against them. (Perhaps
the fighting, which had seemed so admirable, was no
more than a disguised chafing?) I sensed that this kind
of acceptance was not a resigned 'whatever will be will
be' but willing co-operation with Jesus which would en-
able him to lead me further into the different construc-

* Mary Craig *Blessings* (Hodder & Stoughton 1979). By permission.

tive learning experiences he intended through adversity.
Each step was linked to the next; accepting became
resting, resting enabled me to be receptive to learning,
learning offered increasing enrichment in Jesus, and as
I grew in learning I would also be more able to differentiate between the times when it was important to fight,
and the times when I must lie still.

That afternoon, relaxing in the quietness, I could see
the sequence in theory, like a lesson laid out on a black-
board. I hadn't lived it yet, only recognized its importance, though this was the first vital step, giving promise
of more to follow in time, as I became able to understand
and so genuinely respond. In fact the gradual aspect of
the sequence appealed because, by nature, I was cautious
about instantaneous solutions. That was not to say an
immediate and complete 'entering in' was impossible,
but more often it seemed to be a gradual progression, at
least in my own experience. Was God less honoured by a
gradual progression? Weren't both forms of experience
entirely of him anyway?

Throughout the afternoon, while busy with these different thoughts, I'd been waiting for the surgeon again,
but when he did come he talked of everything else except
my going home. And tomorrow was Wednesday, the so-
important goal I had set myself. Why had he delayed
letting me go? Why had the predicted 'three or four
days' now stretched on into a whole week? I wanted to
put the question, but hesitated lest the surgeon should
resent my impatience and think of it as lack of gratitude
for all he was carefully doing to restore my strength. So
I merely smiled in response, and soon he was on his way
down the corridor to see other patients. Maybe he would
return next morning and say, 'How about leaving us this
afternoon?' Surely he would now that I was eating again
and feeling so much better? Then I'd still be home in
time for the twins' birthday tea! I encouraged the
thought to go round and round in my mind in order to
trigger fresh hopefulness, and I was still considering the
possibility when Les came in on his way home from
work. It was suppertime and I had been served a sizeable

cheese salad. He was glad to see me eating.

'Well done! You'll soon be home!'

'Yes, maybe even tomorrow! Will you pick me up after work?'

'Okay, but only if the surgeon gives you the go-ahead.'

We chatted on. Les had bought chips and black puddings from the village shop for the previous night's supper. 'Because we've run out of baked beans,' he admitted.

'Run out of baked beans? But there were nine tins on the shelf and I only put beans twice on your menu list!'

'Yes I know. But we decided to branch out a little on our own, ring a few changes. And somehow the beans have gone.'

Ring a few *changes*? They'd soon be looking like beans! I certainly did need to get home to the family. Les's comment made me all the more determined and he left me in a hopeful, buoyant mood. The sadness, still present deep down, was temporarily forgotten in the pleasure of keeping my eyes fixed on this one immediate goal. 'This time tomorrow I may well be home with the family!'

Determined to get my legs working more efficiently, I walked down the ward corridor for some after-supper exercise and noticed Irene was back from the operating theatre at last, her room full of paraphernalia. I could hardly see her small, thin form in the bed and suddenly felt full of renewed anxiety for her. What had they found? What had they done? Was she going to get better? Completely better? I felt sad to think I wouldn't be able to talk with her again but then remembered prayer could still be an effective means of reaching out and helping her. Maybe Jesus had given Irene to me to care for in this particular way? I thought specially of her when settling for sleep that evening asking that, despite all, she might 'feel after God and find him' in her sorrow. How great her suffering was. Far greater than mine.

6

A New Seeing

'We still need to keep an eye on you,' the surgeon explained next morning. I knew that meant staying in
hospital a little longer, and could feel myself giving in to
immediate self-pity, but then I thought, 'Maybe it will
only be one more day?' and this possibility helped counteract the keen disappointment. Also, the morning post
brought a cheerful letter from Anne, full of village news. I
read it over two or three times and enjoyed visualizing
the fun of school sports day, and the commotion on the
High Street corner where they were breaking up the
road yet again. 'More cables or something, so they say!'
Anne's letter took me right out of myself. It couldn't
have arrived at a better moment. Oh, and she'd collected
the cake too. 'Blue icing and a cream filling.' The last
line of her letter caught my attention. It was a quote
from another of Frances Ridley Havergal's books: 'I
bring my patient God a patient heart'.

Could I do that? Could I let him *be* patience to me,
thus giving himself his own gift? I was not sure. A
theoretical wanting was present, but what about a practical wanting with my whole heart? That was much harder, a stage I had not yet reached.

My thoughts switched quickly back to the family. Had
the boys had time to open their cards and gifts before
leaving for school? Or maybe they were keeping everything until later in the hope of my being there to share
the fun? I knew Les was waiting for my promised phone

97

message, so got up and made the call. 'Sorry, but I won't be coming home today after all.'

Les paused. 'Never mind, I'll come and see you as usual after work and we'll plan a second celebration when you *do* come back to us all!'

That day, a week since my admission (though it seemed much longer), I kept thinking of home. Soon I would be able to sit outside on the back lawn listening to the river's soft murmuring and the joyous song of a rising skylark, and the wind would be full of the scent of flowers. How I enjoyed picturing the scene over and over again in my mind!

Several visitors called that afternoon and evening, and Les spent a while with me after work. Each helped the long day to pass. But in the empty silence after they had all gone the same wretched fear tried to push back into the forefront of my mind. Fear of the future and of a recurrence of the problem, meaning more hospitalization; fear as to whether I would ever reach a settled calm again. And, mingled with the fear, sorrow. A sadness which could not be dismissed for long.

By now, at the end of a slow, hot day I was very weary, but it was impossible to sleep. As the hours dragged by fear tugged the more at my mind and I knew I must somehow escape its powerful onslaught. I remembered the stereo headphones and large selection of cassette music which Lorimer had sent in that afternoon. How about choosing a concert, making up my own programme? Very quietly, in the shadowy semi-darkness, I selected Vivaldi's 'Four Seasons' as the first item, then closed my eyes and lay back.

I felt myself being caught up in the grandeur of it all, released from my small confining world so I could begin to enter into a whole new spacious freedom. A place where, with clearer understanding, I might discover much more of God's good purpose for me.

As my mind relaxed I realized that God delighted to encourage us with occasional glimpses into a world beyond our full understanding. I didn't want to open my eyes and see only the darkness and the plain, clean

ordinariness of the hospital room. I didn't want to
struggle all over again with sadness and fear. Instead I
longed to cling tightly to so joyous an experience so it
could never fade. It was then, when confronted with the
contrast between my present small, confining world and
a sudden vivid glimpse into a new freedom and understanding, that the thought of this writing came to mind.
Not a forceful compulsion, but simply a quiet inner
'knowing'. It was something I needed to do. That was
all.

I needed to try to find out how suffering (any suffering, not just my own small share) could be better understood, even accepted, in the light of a greater purpose
and fulfilment. Suffering still seemed such an enigma. I
wanted to fight it, break free, escape. Yet maybe that
wasn't always possible, nor even helpful in the ultimate
purpose of God? Perhaps he had something far more
valuable for me, and for others who were suffering,
which could not be ours without this intensely painful
prelude. We could only see the sad baffling 'now' while
God considered the whole carefully ordered sequence
of events, leading to the final triumphant culmination.

Not that he was in any way distant or uninvolved with
the turmoiled 'now' of our lives. He felt intensely for us,
suffering even as we suffered, yet at the same time he
was reaching out to support and lead us on into enrichment if only we would hold firmly to his hand. It was so
deep and magnificent a truth! I wanted to apply it more
and more to my own circumstances, and also to try to
record different thoughts, feelings, longings, and small
discoveries so that, by doing so, I would not only find a
measure of inward relief but also begin to recognize
more of the pattern, more of the purpose. Maybe too,
such a sharing through writing would one day offer a
new bond with others in their suffering, and even help
them to reach out towards enrichment too? I did not
know. That possibility was still too far ahead.

*   *   *

'When can I go home?' I asked the surgeon next morning.

'We didn't think you were ready,' he said, smiling in sympathy when he saw my face fall. Then he began to reconsider my request. 'How do you feel about it yourself?'

'I can't wait to be back with the family! I'll be able to rest too . . .'

'Perhaps we'll let you go home tomorrow then.'

'Can't I go tonight? My husband could collect me on his way home from work.'

'Well, we'll see!'

He let me go home that evening. Les reached the hospital by 5.30 p.m., then drove me back through the busy streets and out along the quiet country lanes. I could hardly speak, I was so full of relief and joy! Such a kaleidoscope of greens to delight in too! The green of a grassy hillslope field, the green of new leaves unfolding on late-opening trees, the green of newly-cut hay laid down against already sprouting stubble, the deep, shadowy green of distant hills.

And then we reached home!

'Look, the pansies!' I cried, pulling at Les's arm. They were already in flower, each jostling the next in the plastic trough beside the front step.

'There's another bloom on the Ena Harkness rose too!' Les told me, enjoying my delight. 'But you're not going round to the side garden to see it. I'll bring you a bud later.' And with that he lifted me slowly into his arms and walked straight up to the quiet bedroom. Very tired, but still excited, I lay back and gazed out on the soft trembling green of the far woods. A cool, refreshing, life-giving green. Such a contrast to the sterile white of a hospital ward, the threatening ever-presence of grey disease.

Oh, but it was good to be home! To hear the clatter of dishes downstairs, the sound of voices and laughter, the leap of footsteps up the stairs.

'Look Mum! Here's some birthday cake for you!' Stuart brought me a late tea, then hurried off again. 'I'm just going to fetch my new spanner set to show you. It's great!'

Miss Puss walked purposefully into the room and leapt straight onto the bed then, with a disinterested glance in my direction, she kneaded her own new nest in the candlewick spread, curled herself into a tight black ball, tail over nose, and fell asleep. How far away, how marvellously far away, the hospital seemed!

Sleep was easy that night, away from the night-time bustle of a busy surgical ward. Bright piercing sunlight woke me next morning, and soon afterwards I heard a cuckoo calling. As the day grew hotter thick crowds of gnats gathered above the sycamore trees on the near bank of the river, rising and falling like fragments of gauze fluttering in the breeze. Once Les and the boys had left for work and school, the house became silent but I still had Miss Puss for company as she snored at my feet. Les had left a tray of lunch ready on the bedside table, and I'd promised to stay in the bedroom. But not in bed, so that meant I could enjoy setting out a colourful collection of cards, and watering the many plants and flowers on the window desk. I was surrounded with so much love and concern!

But once these small tasks were done the long morning began to drag. All the previous day's excitement seemed to have drained away and it was frustrating suddenly to be left feeling so low. Why had this happened? I didn't want to admit to my depression, but it was there, heavy and dark, a mingling of physical weakness with mental and spiritual dejection.

I lay down, looking out at the far sunlit woods, and thought back to the few long ago occasions when, trying to project myself into a serious illness situation, I had decided, 'If I ever become ill with something sinister I'll immediately use it as an opportunity to demonstrate my faith. I'll remain steady and calm, an example to others.' I really had thought like that, but how ridiculously smug such confidence seemed now, how the remembrance of it embarrassed me. I had known so little, having no conception at all of the profound disturbance such an illness inevitably provokes. Genuine, steady calm was a far from spontaneous response. It could only be discovered in the midst of long, hard suffering and even then the discovery was likely to be transitory. I would have to search again and find again, and once more draw on new supplies of comfort and strength. But each time the discovery would make those resources the more mine, graces to be gradually possessed rather than briefly borrowed . . .

But I couldn't think long about any discovering and possessing that morning, feeling too bewildered even to reach out towards such things. Why was I experiencing marked physical weariness after the least exertion? Why that hard-to-define feeling of unwellness? (Not clearcut illness. It was not as bad as that.)

I was trying to shake off this black depression when a 'Hallo!' from Anne sounded up the stairs. It was such a pleasure to see her!

'I've come to collect your family's laundry,' she explained. 'Oh, and I've put a chocolate cake in the kitchen.'

Her thoughtfulness cheered me up and it was helpful to talk while Anne perched on the end of the bed.

'Now just you rest back,' she said firmly, 'and content yourself with "being" rather than "doing" for a while. Agreed? We're all standing by to get on with the "doing" for you.'

I frowned, for it was hard to submit to orders, but most of all I appreciated Anne's concern for my wellbeing.

'I'll be back again tomorrow!' she called over her shoulder as she set off with the bulging plastic bag of laundry.

Minutes later a car drew up outside. The front door opened and there were heavier steps on the stairs. It was our doctor. I valued his cheerful greeting and also the sympathy and care he showed when he noticed how I was feeling. After I'd referred briefly to my disappointment at such slow progress, he explained that the weakness was to be expected because the second operation had not been as straightforward as the surgeon anticipated. 'It wasn't a small procedure at all, and the recovery time is bound to take longer as a result,' the doctor told me. As he spoke I began to understand why I had been feeling so unwell and this helped to ease the frustration.

'Now, as for follow-up . . .' our doctor continued. 'You *won't* need any further treatment!'

Oh, what a huge relief! It hit me with full, eager force. No drugs, no radiotherapy, nothing. It was marvellous news! All along this possibility must have been a contributory factor to my fear, though I had deliberately dismissed such thoughts on the few occasions they tried to trouble me.

'However, the surgeon and I have planned follow-up blood tests every three months, and a twice-yearly liver scan . . .'

I tried to listen to the doctor's words but all the time my mind kept repeating, 'no more treatment'. It was so good to know this!

'We'll keep a careful eye on how things go,' the doctor said as he left, and I felt grateful for such reassurance. Who could have asked for more thorough care?

Soon afterwards Helen called, bringing young Peter. It was fun to listen to a small child's chatter again and to watch as he explored under the bed, behind the arm-chair, and up onto the dressing-table stool. It was good of Helen to spare me time in the midst of a busy day. 'I'll buy you some fish when the Macduff van calls round on Tuesday,' she offered. 'What would you like?' The thought of an extra-fresh haddock fillet from up north was too tempting to resist. It would be a great treat!

Later I enjoyed the small flask of vegetable soup Les had made for my lunch and then tried reading a maga-zine, writing two short letters, and listening to music on Radio 3, but the heavy sadness kept trying to press back against my mind.

I tried reading some verses from Isaiah:

> Fear not, for I am with you,
> be not dismayed, for I am your God;
> I will strengthen you, I will help you.
> I will uphold you with my victorious right hand
> (Is 41:10).

The comfort of those strong statements reached deep into my thinking, but it was hard to keep hold of it for long. The heavy blackness was too insistent and, in my weakness, I began to give in.

Another car stopped outside, a heavy-sounding vehicle, not at all familiar. Then a voice called up the stairs. Betty's voice! Could she really have motored all the way across from Stonehaven? Oh what joy, and how exactly right that so close a friend should have come on that particular afternoon!

Betty was laden with fresh lettuces and a large cucumber from their greenhouse (ideal for the salads I loved!) and had also brought a small sachet of lavender tucked into a lace-edged handkerchief. A sweet-smelling touch which I knew I would treasure. Then Betty sat on the bed and talked about happenings at Stonehaven as well as sharing photos of the grandchildren and describing the latest good books she'd read and reviewed. Time with Betty was just what I needed that day and I felt refreshed by her visit, comforted by the concern she showed. I realized she was aware of my thinness and obvious weakness so I deliberately made light of the matter. 'Just you wait, I'll soon be bouncing around again!'

Betty smiled and bent to kiss me. 'Sorry, I have to go, but I'll come again when you're stronger.'

'Oh, please do! How about a coffee date?'

Betty paused. 'Well, we'll see.'

'No, let's make a definite plan,' I insisted. 'Then I'll have something to look forward to.'

So Betty agreed on a midweek morning a fortnight later, and I wrote it in my diary so there'd be a future date to anticipate happily. That was important. It gave me an event to work towards, like a small stepping-stone away from my illness and into normality again.

Tears came to my eyes when Betty left but I quickly blinked them back, embarrassed that I should weep so readily. Murray ambled in from school at 3.30 p.m. and as soon as the back door opened Miss Puss leapt up from the bed and bounded down to greet him, intent on

purring him into giving her an early tea. Les and Stuart
reached home by 6 p.m. and soon the living area downstairs was alive with three deep voices teasing, joking,
questioning, instructing, objecting. I could hear snatches
of their conversation through the open bedroom door
and enjoyed the ordinariness of it all. Thoughts of the
hospital faded still further from my mind. It already
seemed distant, like another world. I was home to stay
now. Surely there would be no need to leave the family
again? I remembered Rachel was due to arrive on the
later bus, eager for a weekend away from the city. It
would be good now to listen in a detached way to her
chatter about the department. Her phone call the previous evening revealed she'd been screening pre-operative chests all week. 'Such a miserable bore!'

By eleven o'clock that night the evening sky had turned
to deep mauve, empty even of birds. Everything was
calm, only the river's quiet song broke the silence. I
wanted to rest back and sleep (Les was already fast
asleep beside me) but, alone with my thoughts, the
sombre blackness again swelled to large, overwhelming
proportions. I could not define it except as that same
sinister power pressing, pressing, pressing against my
mind, squeezing out all of the previous day's easy hope
and mocking my determined attempts to recapture its
joy. That night I felt helpless, completely vulnerable, yet
surely prayer could still be a refuge?

'Lord, thank you because I still have *you*. Help me to
cling to you and so find a safe shelter where the darkness
cannot intrude.'

I heard the village clock strike its single one o'clock
note across the silent streets. Then I fell asleep.

*   *   *

The weekend was busy. There were all kinds of comings
and goings in our upstairs bedroom on Saturday morning. Rachel spent a while at the desk, compiling menus
and shopping lists, then Stuart came in, eager to show
me the Shetland photos which had just arrived in the

post. Murray followed, bringing binoculars with which
to glimpse red squirrels from the window, maybe some
ducks too. Then, when the youngsters had gone, Les
came and lay across the bottom of the bed, content to
answer a barrage of questions about his work. I loved to
hear him talk about it even though my mind could not
readily grasp the technical aspects of gas flow monitoring.

Just before lunch Les went down to fry chips while
Rachel concocted ice cream sundaes. I was sitting and
looking out at the woods when a huge billow of black
smoke suddenly rose up just beyond the window. I flung
back the bedclothes and was about to attempt a rapid
escape downstairs when the thought came, 'If anything
was really wrong they'd have shouted out to me!' so I
relaxed and settled back. Soon afterwards Les arrived
with my soup, looking a little sheepish.

'Did you see a hint of smoke just now?'

'Well, yes, quite a cloud of it actually.'

'The chip pan got a bit overheated. Didn't catch alight
though, so I put it out on the path beside the strawberry
patch.'

We laughed quite a bit over that. You never knew
what was going to happen next when all the family was
home. Later, as evening crept in across the fields, I
listened to another cassette—'Sound of Living Waters'
—letting the fresh, vivid words and melodies reach into
my mind and heart. Such music lifted me up, by-passing
all the dull, tangled thinking and instead offering the
quiet inner delight of worship. David Watson had spoken
of this too, during the radio interview a few months
before, explaining how he'd found music (especially
hymn-singing) invaluable during times when he was too
ill and tired to think or pray. It had helped to lift him to
Jesus. I was glad he'd mentioned this for now I could
take up the suggestion and find new strength through
worship too.

While listening I looked out at the sky, seeing how it
had changed to a pale translucent blue after the shim-
mering heat of the summer's day. The tall Scots pine on
the far river bank was completely still, its thin topmost

branches pointing west into the twilight. Two ducks
passed, beating their way downriver towards the 'Shakkin'
Briggie', high and black against the sky, and a single
moth kept fluttering back and forth outside the window.
Those moments of stillness and reflection had been
much-needed, leaving me at peace.

In the quietness I was able again to consider Jesus'
extreme tenderness, to sense the wonder of his being
there with me in that quiet room, even within me in the
deep hidden places of my mind and heart which no
person could know or understand. I knew that such
tender love and complete identification was the more
dear to me now, after the previous night's turmoil. Why
the turmoil? I didn't know, except that it was an inevitable part of suffering. An illness tried a person on all
fronts. (I had never known, never understood that before,
even after four years of nursing.) I sensed, too, that the
turmoil would try me again, but the rest and refreshment
of the evening's worship had given new resources with
which to counter the onslaught.

Next morning, Sunday, Les and I lingered over our
usual early cup of tea and it was helpful to talk about
some of my feelings with him, though I played down
fears, anxious not to recapture the blackness in words.
One day I would be able to share more fully with him,
but for the moment it was all too raw and painful. As we
talked I wondered again what it would be like to face
suffering alone, not knowing to turn and find refuge in
Jesus. My mind went back to Irene in hospital.

'I don't think we can even imagine the fear and bewilderment Irene must have been facing,' I commented to
Les, picturing her alone in her room on that morning of
the operation. 'What kind of thoughts go through a
person's mind at a time like that? Would they be, "Look
what's happened. If there's a God and he's allowed this
suffering to happen, how can he possibly love me? He
could have prevented it . . ."? I wouldn't have blamed
Irene for thinking like that. From a human point of view
it's an understandable, reasonable reaction. But how
could I have helped her?'

Les hesitated, working out an answer in his mind.

'Surely it's back to the fact that we've all gone wrong and chosen to turn away from God?' He paused again. 'Suffering has resulted. It's the inevitable consequence and will go on and on until God makes a "new heaven and a new earth".'

'Yes, that's true, but how would such a fact help Irene who's right in the middle of hard personal suffering?'

'Well, you'd need to explain that Jesus suffered too, in a far greater way than anyone else. By being crucified he was standing in for every other person, actually being punished in their place in order for them to be brought back to God and so be safe. I think Christ really does know, more than anyone else, what intense suffering feels like.'

'Do you think, too, that in a very definite way he also suffers with us in our own particular anguish?'

'Yes, I'm sure that's so.'

'And also that his pain not only brings us back to God when we accept forgiveness, but also makes it possible for us to invite Jesus right *into* ourselves, so that even if the worst were to happen we'd still be safe? We'd still have shelter in him?'

'Yes, that's true, and very important too. Haven't you been finding it so yourself?'

'I'm beginning to.'

We fell silent, our thoughts moving off in separate directions. I remembered how close Jesus was. How close he always would be, such was his detailed identification. And he was close to Irene too. Was she able to feel this? Did it comfort, even move her to respond in love and longing? Had the strong compassion of Christ at last begun to override any earlier indignation and misguided blame? I prayed that it might be so.

The district nurse came that Sunday morning, just after the family had left for church. The stitches were due to be taken out and I was glad to be rid of them, though found myself strongly resenting the red, puckered scar, directly over the previous incision. 'I guess it will fade in time,' I told myself. 'And then I'll almost forget it's there.'

'You'll be out sunbathing in your bikini yet!' the district
nurse laughed. 'Just the weather for it today!'

When she had gone I spent a while watching two gulls
high in the cloudless sky, circling together in a thermal.
Both were completely black for a few moments, then a
sudden, intense white as their broad wings turned to
catch the sun. An exquisite sight! So restful to watch.
Gazing out on beauty really was therapeutic. Looking
over towards the river I noticed that the single poplar on
the far bank was now covered in opening buds, each
newborn leaf trembling, even in the faintest breeze.

By late evening that same Sunday my room was full of
the scent of stocks. Lin had sent a large bunch from her
country garden (Murray brought them home in a plastic
noodle pot and a carrier bag, dangling from his bicycle
handlebars), and their sweet fragrance brought back
vivid childhood memories of schooldays in Malta. It was
fun to relive them all over again, remembering occasions
when, lessons over, I had rushed towards the city bus
station in the hot midday sun, careful to take the route
which led past a black-dressed flower lady and her colourful stall. Standing there, surrounded by flowers, I
would stop to count the coins in my pocket, hoping for
enough change from the bus fare given by my mother
that morning to buy the largest possible bunch of stocks
—always stocks. If there was sufficient money I'd choose
my bouquet then hurry for the waiting bus, guarding
the flowers and sniffing their strong spicy scent as a
welcome alternative to the garlic-breath of passengers
crowded in alongside. I could hardly wait to reach the
bus stop near our home, then run along the harbour
wharf, across the road, through the high gates, and up
the stone steps to find my mother and offer my gift. I
had always been so sure she would be pleased, so sure
she would say, 'Oh, are those for me? What a surprise!'
And inside myself I'd be bursting with the pride and
pleasure of giving her so special and unexpected a present. It never occurred to me that my mother had borne
the entire cost, thus giving herself her own gift, nor had

she ever shown anything other than total surprise and
delight.

Stocks would always be evocative! Our own seedlings
were still small but Les had reported finding a few buds.
I couldn't wait to be up and about, able to admire the
new flower border and search for the first strawberry.
Les had already harvested a row of radishes and one or
two lettuces, and from the upstairs window I could see
that the small vegetable plot was looking healthy, though
the carrot seeds had failed to germinate. Several cabbage
white butterflies were in evidence too, fluttering over
our single row of cabbage seedlings with immense ma-
ternal satisfaction.

*   *   *

Monday morning brought silence to the house as everyone dispersed, but not before setting me up for the day.
I was being thoroughly spoiled, and though this was
temporarily enjoyable, I knew the pleasure would soon
wear thin. Then I would want to be up and doing. When
could I go downstairs? When would I be able to help
around the house?

'Not yet,' Les kept insisting. 'Not for a long time yet.'
But I hoped it would be soon.

Around midmorning I heard a child's voice on the
stairs. Shonagh, from a few doors down, had brought
Emma to visit. 'And I thought you might like a tea break
too!' she said, setting a tray down beside me. How
thoughtful of her! She had laid it with her best china,
adding milk, sugar and biscuits. 'Emma chose the biscuits!'

I felt moved by such detailed concern, and the more
so on a busy Monday morning. Shonagh sat and talked
for a few minutes, bringing me up to date with neigh-
bourhood news. Then, 'Are you doing better now?' she
asked, a frown crossing her face.

'Yes, I'm getting along just fine!'

It was easier to be brief and paint a bright picture.
Doing so avoided the necessity for further explanations
and would also, I hoped, put Shonagh at ease. In fact I

used the phrase 'getting along just fine' without even
thinking, and only later, when Emma's happy chatter
had faded into the distance and the front door had
closed, did I stop to realize my lack of honesty. Wouldn't
it have been better to say, 'Yes, I'm much better, but
there are still some hard times'? That was more truthful.
Perhaps I should reply like that next time?

Anne arrived an hour later.

'I've come to change the sheets,' she explained and
though I objected, not wanting to give her extra Monday
morning work, she remained insistent, her mind made
up. She had also brought all of the previous week's
laundry back, neatly ironed and folded. How good
friends were! How would I ever be able adequately to
express my gratitude?

'I need to make a business phone call to London,' I
told Anne, remembering an editor was awaiting a response to an article request. 'So I'll just go downstairs for
a few minutes, then when I get back I'll help you make
the bed.'

'You won't help with the bed, and you're not going
downstairs on your own.' Anne looked me straight in
the eye, then she softened. 'Let's go down together. I'll
help you.'

It was embarrassing to be dependent in this way and
even more so to discover my shakiness when we reached
the stairs. I felt annoyed and impatient with myself, yet
grateful for Anne's help. It was a relief eventually to lie
back between the cool clean sheets and rest.

'Friends around the village keep asking after you,'
Anne said.

'Do they?' I was amazed, also much humbled by their
thoughtfulness. 'Tell them I'm doing well, won't you.'

'I'll tell them you're making slow progress,' Anne said.

Several more neighbours called during the day—
Annette, Ruth, Shirley, Mhairi. Each helped the day to
pass and sometimes I felt very moved by their kindness.
I was aware that friends were uncertain about what to
say when they came into the room. They glanced at me,
sized up the situation, then responded in one of a few

different ways. Most sat straight down and commented
on Lin's stocks, the Ena Harkness rosebud, or the wide
view from the window. Then we chatted on about village
news.

I enjoyed such conversations, wanting to be as involved
as ever with all that was happening, and relieved not to
have to refer to myself at all. Yet at the same time I
didn't mind being asked. If a friend chose, from uneasiness, not to ask questions, then I accepted and welcomed
her avoidance. If another walked in and immediately
enquired, 'How are you feeling today?' then I could use
my brief, prepared answer. 'Better, thank you. But . . .
it's still a bit hard at times.' Usually the matter rested
there as the friend continued with another topic. 'How
are Les and the boys managing?' 'It's a beautiful day,
isn't it!' 'Can I buy you anything at the supermarket?'
Once or twice a visitor replied, 'Yes, I suppose it's bound
to be hard. You've been through quite a lot. Two operations in a very short time . . .' and then we moved on to
another subject.

Sometimes, however, friends like Anne, Helen or
Mhairi must have sensed that more lay behind my, 'it's a
bit hard at times' phrase and started to feel the matter
out, letting me talk on if I wanted to do so. Their concern meant a great deal to me. It was not an offensive
probe at all, merely a straightforward, 'In what way is it
hard? Can I help you?' But although I often longed to
be able to answer, I couldn't yet explain inner feelings in
any detail. There was still too much of a muddle churning
around beneath the surface of my mind. I was aware of
it but couldn't face it, so instead tried to steer clear of the
matter most of the time by giving a non-commital answer,
'Oh, it's nothing really! I'll soon get over it.'

I hoped, however, that even though Anne, Helen and
Mhairi hadn't received much of a response to their gentle
questioning, they would still keep this level of communi-
cation open. I needed it. One day I would find words for
all the hidden bewilderment and then it would be a
great relief to release it. I sensed, too, that there was
something very specific but as yet indefinable, which had

to be expressed sooner or later. But I was not ready yet. Over and over again I wondered if others in similar circumstances felt like this. Did they know what I was referring to? If only someone could have come up alongside and defined and explained it to me.

The best times of all during those days spent upstairs were the long summer evenings when, home from work and school, Les and the lads would come up to chat and joke with me. The boys didn't stay long (there was always so much to entice them outside during summertime), but Les would remain and together we'd look out of the window, noticing the changes each unfolding summer's day brought.

'The hawthorn is coming into blossom at last!' I told Les on one such evening.

'About time too. Maybe the wet spring set it back.'

Then we sat watching several swifts skimming low and fast over the river, scooping up billfuls of insects and, as night fell, I noticed the sky was cobbled with small grey clouds. When I pointed this out to Les he sized the matter up with his seasoned pilot's eye and said, 'Looks as if some weather is coming!'

Rain was a welcome possibility after so many long hot days. Murray had already tried hosing down the garden earlier in the evening, eager for an excuse to douse everything else in sight—car, bicycles, cat, windows, lawn mower, tea towels on the washing line. He had soaked himself too, of course, and later left a trail of muddy puddles right through the house.

Next morning I decided to spend the day concentrating on praising God by way of contrast to my recent spiritual dullness. The idea came from a verse Les and I had read, telling of how Asaph and his colleagues had been given 'the responsibility for singing praises to the Lord' (1 Chron 16:7 GNB). Whoever would have thought of praise as a *responsibility*? I'd always considered it to be a when-I-feel-like-it response, and I hadn't felt at all like praising lately. 'If I willed myself to praise God rather than waiting for the rare feeling to come would it make any difference?' I wondered. 'Would it help keep my fear and sadness under control?' These thoughts kept running through my mind as I deliberately gave myself to enjoyment (all kinds of enjoyment) throughout the day. I listened to different types of music, read a few chapters of an Elizabeth Goudge novel, started on a simple knitting project, and then spent a long while lying back to gaze and gaze on beauty—trees, birds, blossom, the ever-moving river.

As I did so I realized again how important it was to stop and be still, to look out onto loveliness. Not just during a time of illness or convalescence either, but in the midst of any day. It was vital, and thinking of this made me regret my previous flustered over-activity which had inevitably denied me the richness of such pauses. Would I still be responsive to moments of quietness and beauty later on, after returning to a full programme? Would my nature be generous enough? Words written by Robert Louis Stevenson came to my mind and I found them jotted down in a notebook on the bedroom desk: 'Extreme busyness, whether at school, kirk or market, is a symptom of deficient vitality ... It is no good speaking to such people, they *can not* be idle, their nature is not generous enough.'* A blunt statement, hitting quite hard. But the more valuable for that reason.

Late that night I made a praise list in my mind and stopped to thank God for so many good things:

— a quiet, calm, happy day,
— the freshness of our garden after the previous night's rain,
— the surprise delivery of a beautiful bouquet from Bournemouth,
— Shonagh calling in again to bring me morning coffee and afternoon tea,
— my friend Mhairi's unexpected arrival with delicious home-made chicken broth for my lunch,
— the pleasure of seeing our minister and another friend, John, when they called in,
— the happiness of Les's homecoming from work and the boys' exuberant arrival back from school,

* Robert Louis Stevenson *Virginibus Puerisque*.

— the close, increasingly real presence of God, his continuing patience with me.

Gladness and praise *had* made the day different! The Chronicles verse might have appeared obscure and unrealistic at first glance but now I could readily accept its important relevance. Whatever my circumstances there was still plenty of cause for gratitude, laying upon me the welcome responsibility of giving praise to God. Praise had helped to relieve the mental and spiritual weariness too, at the same time having a happy effect upon my physical condition. There had been all kinds of surprise benefits!

A few days later I pleaded with Les to let me join him downstairs for supper and at last he relented. The lads were both out so we enjoyed an hour to ourselves by the fireside (it was damp and cold outside), eating scrambled eggs and chatting about plans for coming weeks. The school holidays were due to start a few days later and in August Rachel would be home for her summer break too. The house would be fairly humming with activity! Maybe we could drive over to visit Les's relatives in Pitlochry? And perhaps we should take our minister up on his generous offer of the caravan for a few days? Les was about to start on permanent shift hours, working an eighty-four hour week followed by seven days at home. We would be able to go away together during his off-duty week!

It was exciting to plan different goals. Each was important. The first was looming ahead less than a week later when I planned to join church friends at our Bible study group's 'Summer Lunch'. It was always a highlight of the year together. Then there was a young friend, Catherine's, wedding in early July and maybe a caravan holiday a few weeks later. Eager anticipation of these different events was already helping me to move out beyond the immediate situation. Without such goals I would have fallen prey to much more frequent self-preoccupation. I knew it would give particular satisfaction to reach each milestone too, for the sequence marked a slow, steady return to normality. The evening's brief

time downstairs had been a first milestone. It felt extra
good to leave the bedroom behind for a while. Later,
when physical weariness returned, Les helped me upstairs and I lay enjoying the sight of three herons flapping
slowly home across the silver sky.

*   *   *

As the days went by I began to value opportunities for
talking at length with those who came to visit. Mhairi
called one morning, 'just to chat!' but also to say how
she'd recently been learning to acknowledge and recognize the value side of suffering.

'It all appeared to be a complete muddle before, with
no purpose at all,' she explained. 'Now I'm beginning to
see that God can use a very hard time to bring blessing
into our lives. And perhaps we wouldn't be able to experience such blessing in any other way.'

'What sort of blessing?'

'Well, the blessing of finding out how much we need
God. Suffering humbles us, doesn't it? Makes us realize
we can't manage our lives alone; we haven't got all the
answers. Something deep inside forces us to reach out
towards Jesus and there's no peace till we've found him.
Really found him, I mean, in the sense of giving our
problem, and even our whole lives over to him . . .'
Mhairi trailed off, then she suddenly sat forward in the
armchair. 'My, but how I'm going on today! You'll be
thinking I'm preaching or something!'

'No, I'm not thinking that at all. It's true, through
suffering you really do find out how much you need
Jesus . . .' Mhairi insisted on going downstairs to make
us both some coffee and, while we were sipping it, read
me a psalm she'd been studying during the week:

> But I have calmed and quieted my soul,
> like a child quieted at its mother's breast;
> like a child that is quieted is my soul
>
> (Ps 131:2).

Such a simple picture yet vivid with meaning! After
Mhairi had gone I spent a while recalling her words
about suffering, and then going over the psalm verse in
my mind. It had been helpful to have time to talk over
significant thoughts and discoveries. My present circumstances were deepening our friendship, opening up new
levels on which to share. Surely this, in itself, was also
part of the value side of suffering?

That same morning one of our teenage friends, Julie,
arrived with some shortbread and a sponge her mother
had baked for us. Then a neighbour called to deliver a
large lettuce and another friend also visited, bringing a
tin of sweets. How blessed I felt! Much humbled, too, to
be now so often on the receiving end of kindness. Sometimes though I longed to be out and about, busy with my
usual 'doing' role. Then Anne's admonition, 'Content
yourself with just "being", would come back to my mind.
She was right. Nonetheless, 'being' didn't seem very
satisfactory. It didn't appear to make any constructive
outward contribution. I would far rather have been able
to 'do'. And, in fact, there were still legitimate things I
could, and needed to do. I began work on two short
newspaper articles and set myself the task of catching up
on letter-writing at the rate of a couple of letters per
day. The desk drawers and files needed sorting out too,
and once that was done maybe I should plan an un-
demanding writing programme for the coming months?
I was eager to start writing again, but the more complex
project which had come to mind on that last night in
hospital would have to wait. I was not ready for it yet.

Prayer became another 'doing' opportunity. I now
had plenty of time for quiet intercession and felt glad
when people gave me specific needs to share in prayer.
One friend, Elizabeth, was preparing for camp the following month, so supplied me with a list of the girls and
leaders due to participate. This made it possible for me
to pray for two by name each day and I enjoyed having
this small part in all the bustle and excitement of their
approaching camp week. Then, too, 'would you pray for
my neighbour who's just had a bad accident,' Mhairi

asked on one of her visits, and another friend sent a long letter sharing her struggle with depression. 'Please pray for me,' she wrote at the end.

There were so many needs to bring to Jesus in prayer and, as time went by, I began to view intercession in a completely new way. It wasn't an incidental at all, and for this reason it was inappropriate to apologize, as I had often done in the past, with, 'If only I could do more than just pray for you!' *Just* pray? Prayer was a prime responsibility, for by it I could put different people with their different needs (some complex and seemingly insoluble) into the hands of a God for whom nothing was impossible. The growing certainty of this filled me with amazement, greatly increasing my incentive to pray. In fact, how could I not do so when prayer could help to make such a marked difference in a needy person's situation? Of all the 'doing' opportunities during those recuperation days this came to mean most of all.

In many ways I was beginning to move out beyond myself. This was essential, and for the most part, beneficial, except that while reaching out to try to help others I was at the same time refusing to face up to and resolve my own needs. In giving myself as fully as possible to a limited 'doing' programme I was dismissing the mental and emotional aftermath of my illness, attempting to live almost as if the whole thing had never happened. Fear and sadness were deliberately overlaid with activity so I could avoid any confrontation with them, but I did not stop to consider that such avoidance would ultimately make matters far worse.

Only on rare occasions did the inner turmoil break through my carefully-constructed 'doing' barrier, and such times were always unexpected. One occurred the second evening I joined the family downstairs for supper. The phone rang just as we were finishing the meal. It was an English friend, Jayne, making a long-distance call to check on my progress. I appreciated her concern. 'What does it feel like to know you've had cancer?' she asked suddenly.

Although I didn't mind so direct a question the last

word gave me a sharp jolt, perhaps because, in my reluctance to come to terms with having had cancer, I still baulked at any reference to the matter, resisting its implications. 'I don't really know,' I admitted. 'There's something still inside my mind which hasn't yet been accepted or expressed.'

The need to put this inner uneasiness into an answer for Jayne proved strangely helpful. It was a small release. Later, as my mind went back over our conversation, I remembered times during the past few weeks when, without warning, I had felt tears coming to my eyes. On each occasion I had quickly resisted their intrusion, but perhaps weeping was part of the needed expression of bewilderment, almost of hurt, essential to mental and emotional acceptance and recovery? The more I considered this the more likely it seemed, but eventually I set the matter aside, unwilling to follow through on the matter any further.

'And anyway, my own malignancy was so small a thing,' I reminded myself, determined to reconstruct the avoidance barrier.

*   *   *

June ended in an exceptional blaze of heat. On the last Sunday of the month I persuaded Les to take me out for a drive and dressed for the occasion in a pale yellow outfit which he had always admired. It sagged at the shoulders now, but the elasticated waist fitted closely, which reassured me. How good it felt to be wearing daytime clothes and walking out of the front door into the fresh warm air! Les drove along the road to nearby Monymusk and I noticed how the hay had been laid out to dry in the fields along our route. Several daisies and buttercups had started to wither in the stubble, and flocks of oyster-catchers, rooks, and crows were foraging up and down the parallel rows. The lime trees were now in full leaf and an impressive avenue of them shaded us as we approached the village of Keig. Several laburnums were in flower too, each golden cluster bowing to its

partner in the breeze, and further on—along the Lord's
Throat road—we came across pure white rowan blossom
and bank upon bank of mauve and purple rhododen-
drons. I had never seen them in such profuse bloom
before, and there were also clumps of wild flowers
everywhere. Such a delight!

Once home I deliberately took the longer route to the
back door in order to inspect the side garden at leisure.
Les's favourite lupins were in full multi-colour flower
and a new forsythia seemed well established though the
nearby japonica was struggling, being rather over-
shadowed by hollyhocks. One or two mauve stocks were
in full, fragrant bloom too. Beautiful! I hardly dared to
glance at my own particular area of the garden, the back
border. It looked quite a tangle, but petunias and Zinnias
were braving the weeds.

'Come on, no more dilly-dallying!' Les objected when
he saw me stoop to hunt for a first strawberry, but then
he found and picked it for me.

Eleanor, a friend from the west coast, telephoned that
evening, wanting to assure me of her love for us both.
Afterwards she broke down and explained how angry
she had been with God, 'for sending good people such
suffering'. I was baffled, not knowing how to respond,
then started to explain that we were not good apart
from God making us so, and also that he allowed, rather
than sent, suffering.

'Besides, what we've been through is such a small
thing compared to Jesus' suffering,' I tried to point out.
'Even though he was God he had to go through all that
terrible pain, so surely I can learn to accept my own
much smaller part?'

Eleanor was silent for a few seconds.

'Yes, but it all seems so meaningless, so cruel somehow.'

'Not if there's important value to be found despite it
all. And that will happen, just as it happened through
Jesus' pain. In a small way it is happening already. I
can't really put it into words. It's just that I'll never be
quite the same as before.'

We talked on for a little longer. I tried to share some

of Mhairi's thoughts on suffering with Eleanor but she still seemed unconvinced. After her loving, 'Goodbye! I'll be praying for you,' I sat beside the phone for a few minutes reflecting on what Eleanor had said. The fact that she was angry with God on my behalf had come as quite a surprise. Did other friends feel like that too? He had spared me from such anger by helping me gradually to acknowledge the value side of suffering, but nonetheless I was still in the midst of a considerable struggle with bewilderment.

In the quiet of that Sunday evening I began to admit to my bewilderment, at the same time remembering Jesus' nearness to me. And as I thought of his intimate identification with me in my struggles the bewilderment receded for a little while. Until that point I had never really grasped that Jesus loved me in such a total way, waiting for even the slightest response on my part, and so eager to know that I loved and longed for him too. When I thought of him seeking me over and over again with such undeserved tenderness the realization of my frequent indifference filled me with acute shame. How could I in any way hesitate or hold back from him?

It was the first of many further occasions when I would feel constrained to reach out and take him to myself more and more. How could the resulting delight of such a oneness and the accompanying sense of well-being be described, except that it was like falling in love, finding yourself filled full of wonder at belonging to someone who was 'all joy'. Had suffering brought me to this new seeing and understanding? Could there have been, for me, no other way?

> There are places in man's heart which do not yet exist,
> and into them enters suffering,
> so that they may have existence.*

It must have been a few days later, when Anne called for coffee, that I realized how clearly Jesus' picture of

* Leon Boly from Mary Craig *Blessings* (Hodder & Stoughton 1979). By permission.

the vine and its branches illustrated the potential and
beauty of this oneness with him, of his life lived through
ours. Anne brought the subject up, pointing out the
parable in John 15 verses 1–5.

'But is this a once-for-all experience, or a gradual
take-over?' she queried, afraid lest, in speaking of oneness with Jesus, we should presume to have finally 'arrived' with no more learning needed. I shared her cau-
tion, but as we talked further realized the whole concept
indicated a steady entering-in with more and more to be
discovered, yet much to be presently delighted in too.
Christianity was so exciting! Not in any way discouraging.

'To think that there's so much more joy yet to be
experienced!' I commented as Anne stood up to go. 'I'm
beginning to understand it now. But only beginning.'

7

The Crisis of Acceptance

Les's training course with the oil company was going well, and in July he started full-time in the gas flow control room, working shift hours. Soon afterwards his first pay slip came through and at supper time he laid it down by my place at the table. The lads hardly noticed but it was a significant moment for the two of us.

'Incidentally, you'll see the income tax reduction is enough to pay back six weeks of unemployment benefit all in one go,' Les commented, spreading his bread thickly with my home-made strawberry jam.

I understood the implication of his remark, knowing that this single fact would already have greatly eased his mind. He'd found drawing regular benefit payments irksome in the extreme and the effect had lingered on. Perhaps the matter would be completely forgotten now? After our meal Les took the wage slip in his hand and thanked God for all that his provision in this way meant to us. It was a prayer full of praise and joyous meaning.

Glancing at Les across the table I saw again the quiet, happy confidence which had been so sadly missing before. Not that he didn't still hanker for an aircraft flight deck at times. My thoughts went back to an afternoon a few weeks earlier when we'd been driving back from Aberdeen together and Les had taken an unexpected side turn, off the usual route.

'Where are you going?' I'd objected.

'Oh, just along the airport road to see which planes

have come in today . . . I still often dream about flying.'
His answer had come as a surprise. I thought he had
forgotten all about flying. Yet I was glad he'd told me. I
needed to understand. Les wasn't discontented. It was
just that flying was a part of his make-up, and always
would be.

At the first opportunity after the pay slip came we set
off on a family outing.

'This is a three-in-one celebration,' Les explained as
he drove us towards Aberdeen. 'It's for my work, and
your improvement, and the boys' good O-grade results.
Quite a red letter occasion!'

After picking Rachel up in the city we set off south to
the bird sanctuary at Fowlsheugh. It was very hot and a
thick sea mist was already creeping eerily inland by the
time we reached the town of Stonehaven. Les drove past
the attractive old harbour and up the steep side of the
cliff beyond, searching for the sanctuary turning. We
discovered it at last but by then the mist had gathered in
thick white clouds which billowed all around us. Nonetheless we found Fowlsheugh at the end of the narrow
approach lane and, even in the mist, could tell it was an
impressive place. High cliffs fell sharply to the sea below,
their grassy summits carpeted with sea pinks, clover and
vetch, and roughened in places by rocky outcrops, scab-
bed with bright golden lichen. A path led to a prominent
viewpoint from which, through breaks in the mist, we
glimpsed numerous narrow cliff ledges, whitened by
droppings and thronged with gulls, guillemots and
razor-bills. Thousands upon thousands of birds—some
roosting, some preening, some flying, some swimming
and fishing in the calm black water below. Breathtaking!

Later we drove inland to escape the menacing mist
and enjoyed a picnic lunch beside a small gurgling river,
screened by overhanging trees. Rachel talked Les into
giving her some extra driving practice afterwards so we
took the long route home and stopped at the Bridge of
Feugh salmon leap, hoping to see a few fish struggling
upriver to spawn. There wasn't a single salmon in sight,
though we noticed a small dark brown animal creeping

stealthily across the rocks, then sliding into the water.

'I bet it's a mink,' Les said. 'And up to mischief too, no doubt.'

We reached home as the long twilight shadows were stretching far out across upland fields. It had been a good day and there had been no aftermath of weariness. I really was making progress!

In fact by now (a month since the operation), I had begun to help out with cooking and cleaning downstairs and could manage well, provided I took frequent rests. I had been particularly proud of the jam made with our first large picking of strawberries, and also with fruit from a nearby farm. Then an older friend, Rose, insisted on my accepting a bowlful of her homegrown straw-berries when I called to visit one morning. Rose had been on my mind for I knew she'd injured her leg quite badly during a fall, and I'd longed to be able to go and visit her. It gave particular pleasure to be now strong enough to do so and I found her bright, but still experi-encing considerable pain.

'The worst part of all is not being able to get out and about as usual,' Rose told me. 'I feel cut off from people, lonely too. I suppose I've never known what it's like to be a shut-in until now.'

I felt for her, and as we talked on thought again of Linda's visit to the hospital, and her valuable gift of time. I needed still to hold firmly to what, quite unknow-ingly, she had shown and taught me, for it would be easy in the enthusiasm of my recovery, to overlook those who lingered on in loneliness.

Rose's generous bowlful of strawberries enabled me to boil up another pan of jam and, while it was simmering, I started to cut and sew four scarlet-coloured cushions to go with the livingroom carpet. A simple task, but some-how it gave great satisfaction, though the colour seemed much too bright once the new cushions were in place.

'Wow!' Rachel exclaimed when she arrived home next day. 'Whatever made you choose *that* colour, Mum?'

I'd been chiding myself with the same question.

'I guess I bought the stuff in too much of a hurry—

just before going into hospital when my mind was all flustered.'

'You're probably right, Mum,' Rachel answered gently. 'But if you like I'll look around for some different material to tone in with another of the main colours. Something in beige perhaps?'

She was already kneeling on the carpet, head tilted to one side as her artistic eye studied the tile pattern.

'And Mum, you could also make new covers for the stool and the dining table using the same beige material . . . and then how about some curtains too . . . and . . .'

'Steady on, Rachel!' Les protested, glancing up from the newspaper crossword. 'I'm not made of money you know. At least, not yet!'

I smiled to myself, catching the look which passed between them. Les was always quick to jump on Rachel's lavish spending schemes but nonetheless enjoyed a particularly close bond with her, evident again on this occasion as she leapt up to perch on the arm of his chair before snatching the paper out of his hand and dropping it onto the floor.

'Oh Dad, you're always such an old bore! When are you going to get excited about things? When are you going to actually *do* exciting things?'

Then she sidled closer deliberately to tease him with a long description of her latest shopping spree in the city.

'I spent *all* Thursday evening looking round those big stores in Union Street. Of course, I didn't actually buy anything. At least, not very much. Just a new sun top for the summer, and a nice belt, and another pair of sandals . . .'

It did me good to watch them together as I leant back in the armchair opposite and relaxed. I was very tired. Over the past few days there had been some recurrence of dull pain in my right side and with it a degree of nausea. Eating had been difficult, though I still enjoyed fruit and vegetables.

'But those will never help you gain weight,' Les kept objecting. He had bought me a supply of Complan and glucose so I dutifully added both of these to drinks, or

sprinkled them over fruit salads and jellies. I knew I was
still losing weight but hoped no one would notice. Deep
down this troubled me, as did the pain and sickness.
They were frustrating reminders of the illness, and
limiting factors in any attempt to resume as full a programme as possible.

I longed to be right back to normal with every aspect
of the problem left far behind and forgotten, yet I kept
being confronted with lingering weakness and eating
difficulties. Inevitably I became more and more frustrated and the end result was an even greater determination
to keep as busy as possible in order to try to win against
weakness. I just must not give in! It was an unwise and
irrational way to tackle the situation, and I knew it, but
somehow had to keep my mind off the illness and its
associated stress-points. If, by a daily 'doing' programme, I
could still maintain my carefully constructed avoidance
barrier then surely all would work out well in the end.
Surely it would? The question hung, unanswered, in my
mind.

*   *   *

August came, full of the excitement of having all the
family home, yet for some reason I couldn't completely
rid myself of sadness. Not an obvious sadness, more a
heavy inner weight, much as I'd known in hospital many
weeks before. Perhaps it was linked to the continuing
uneasiness in my mind, or perhaps such heaviness was
inevitable while I resisted any confrontation with deep
fears?

Early in the month my mother arrived for a week's
holiday together with my sister, Ros, and her two young
boys. It was fun to visit different sandy beaches together
—Aberdeen, Balmedie, Collieston—and to fly kites, play
on park roundabouts, and wander round the transport
museum. We drove along Donside and Deeside too,
stopping at favourite picnic sites to relive the pleasure of
previous family visits. It was good of Mother and Ros to
motor all the way up from the south to be with us and I
hoped my sadness wasn't in any way apparent to them.

The small boys' liveliness kept it mostly at bay and particularly one teatime when young Rhys had us rocking with laughter. He'd been reprimanded for eating too many chocolate cakes but was not inclined to accept his mother's correction. Instead he beamed up into Ros's face and declared, 'Well, I *can* make myself be even more naughty if you'd like me to!'

How quiet and empty the house seemed the morning they all left. I missed the boys' eager chatter and excited squeals.

'Let's take the car up beyond Tilliefoure,' Les suggested. 'I've some magazines to return to the Phillips.'

It was a clear sunlit morning and Les drove slowly so as not to miss any birds along Donside. We came across a single whooper swan sleeping in the riverside reeds by the Tilliehashlach bend. Later, on our return, it was dabbling nearby, an unusual sight in midsummer. Had the wild swan been left behind by a migrating flock in early spring? Would it rejoin them during their return south in the coming autumn?

'We must keep a look out and see what happens,' Les said.

Just before reaching the village we stopped at an antiques shop to look for a much-needed bookcase, and found one made of oak in an unusual and attractive design.

'It's exactly right!' I told Les, picturing it beside the upstairs desk. Next day I spent a while arranging books on its shelves, amongst them a few from nursing training days. One was a *Textbook of Medicine* and I decided, rather hesitantly, to look up the 'liver diseases' section. The idea had occurred to me once or twice before but I'd deliberately resisted, afraid of what I might find. There were no more than a few brief paragraphs on the condition. The last sentence read: 'Primary neoplasms are rare, but secondary ones are common; and all are incurable.'

I read the sentence once more, taking in each phrase, then quickly shut the book and put it far down on the bottom shelf. 'Things have changed now,' I insisted.

It was a Saturday and after lunch the family seemed to scatter in different directions. Les went out to touch up some rust spots on the car, the boys cycled over to Monymusk to swim in an upstream stretch of the Don, and Rachel set off along the riverside path to look for wild flowers.

'Don't forget to have a long rest,' Les had instructed earlier. 'I'm putting the sun-lounger out on the back lawn.' So I felt obliged to co-operate and soon began to enjoy the quiet, scented loveliness of the summer's afternoon. But the sadness was still there. I could feel its pressure breaking through each careful restraint, to override all else, even the pleasure of such restful surroundings. What was causing it? My mind went back to a poem I had found when writing the book on death so many months before. It had been written by a young woman suffering from a malignant disease:

> There is a sadness growing
> Within me
> I do not want it so, but
> I know
> I cry with bitterness
> Filling me.
> It does not hurt the way
> It did
> Yesterday.
>
> There is only room for
> Just so much sorrow.
> What will I put in
> Its place
> Tomorrow?*

After first reading those words I had been moved by their poignancy. But at that time, almost eighteen months earlier, I had looked at them from the outside, as no more than an observer intrigued by a strange, unfamiliar scene. Now those lines had come to have

* From *To Live Until We Say Goodbye* (Prentice-Hall 1979).

immediate meaning. They reached through to me on every side, searching me out. All those long months before, as I copied out the poem and put together every other part of the small book on suffering and death, I had thought I was writing for others. But all the time, as I listened to people speaking bravely of personal pain and bereavement, as I absorbed and tried to understand, I was learning, learning, learning for myself, though I did not know it. How often their words came back to me now. How often their courage challenged. But they had been open and honest about their pain too, in no way dismissive. They knew 'the sadness growing'. And because they were prepared to talk about it, because their words still lived on in my own mind, perhaps they would now be able to reach through and help me face, even resolve, my own deep need?

I had tried so desperately to dismiss fear and sadness, by erecting a barrier to protect me from them. But eventually this would only prove the more harmful, for fear grew behind such a barrier. I was beginning to recognize this now or, rather, to be willing to recognize it. The barrier had to be dismantled so that the fear might be faced, its cause identified, and a strong counter-active answer found. I began, very tentatively, to approach and consider the sorrowful fear which had lived and grown within me for so long, realizing it to be, in essence, that heavy foreboding about the future. (Would the growth recur? How would it be treated? Would I die?) And the foreboding arose from the fact that I now had to live with a degree of uncertainty, however slight. Such an uncertainty was the more irksome to a clearcut person like me. I had always insisted on knowing exactly where I was now and what was going to happen next before I could allow my mind to rest. I was made that way. How could I change?

There seemed to be no immediate answer. My mind was tired and I felt spent after such a confrontation, broken somehow, and yet not without hope. In time there would be an answer. One day I would discover something more powerful than all else to put in the place of sorrow.

I lay watching a pair of Red Admiral butterflies fluttering above the flower border, then several groups of hungry sand-martins swept back and forth over the grassy river bank, a fleet interweaving of brown and white. Marvellous sight! I remembered other words discovered when gathering material for the book. Words about being broken up, yet still with the certainty of restoration. 'Man is born broken, he lives by mending; the grace of God is glue.'* Yes, there would be a mending. But how? When?

It was then that Rachel strolled back across the grass, climbed the garden stile, and held out her tangled bouquet of wild flowers.

'There are masses and masses along the bank, Mum! You should see them!'

She fetched the wild flower book and we tried to identify most of the drooping blooms before Rachel stood them in a glass of water, ready for sketching and painting. I was glad she planned to capture their fading loveliness in such a way. It would be a lasting record of that summer afternoon's happiness. Perhaps, too, of its first new hope?

That same weekend we drove across country to visit older friends, Tom and Joan, seeing a first harvester at work en route. Les and I spent a while talking with Tom in his quiet study-caravan on the hillside, enjoying the warm fragrant breeze which was blowing in through the open door. At one point Tom spoke of 'vivid Christianity' and the adjective made an immediate impression, for I knew he meant the vividness which always results from a deepening love relationship with Jesus. It couldn't be hidden. It shone out. Tom and Joan certainly lived out a vivid Christianity themselves, though they were quite unaware of the fact. I valued time to listen, observe, and think. Just being with them helped me further to forget the inner heaviness. It was a small event in the midst of a full weekend, perhaps, but I realized God had specifically

* Eugene O'Neill from Mary Craig *Blessings* (Hodder & Stoughton 1979). By permission.

planned this fresh encouragement for me. He was still in control of my situation, still working to turn all its different aspects to value in my life, this fact being the more underlined by the apt timing of such encouragement.

*   *   *

The following morning, after the gladness of being with Tom and Joan, I called at the doctor's surgery for a routine prescription. He welcomed me in and I was glad to report my progress.

'I can do much more now without getting tired, and I'll be out on my bike again before long!'

It seemed a good lead-in before asking a question which had been on my mind for some time. It concerned the three-monthly checks. The thought of regularly attending for these had increased my foreboding. Surely such blood tests weren't necessary if the outlook was so good? But before I could put the question into words the doctor began talking about the operation, explaining that it had been less straightforward than expected because the surgeon had found and removed two or three other small areas of questionable tissue. This information came as a real shock. I had not known anything about it before. And as I sat there in the small hot room I began to understand why further checks were a sensible precaution. There was no need to ask my carefully prepared question.

On my way out into the village High Street and along the road home, all the half-forgotten fear surged back with huge, overwhelming force. Had the problem already spread? Were there still more areas which hadn't been found? Or would some develop in future? What if they did? How would they be treated? Surely it wouldn't mean going into hospital for another operation? I was vulnerable now. The slightest element of uncertainty immediately threw me off-balance, and any tentative thoughts about a new hope were pushed far into the background.

There was plenty to be done at home that busy Monday morning so I worked carefully through the routine, but all the time my mind was in confusion. The more I insisted, 'Don't be so foolish', the more I remembered how unpredictable some malignancies could be. I just could not cope with such an uncertainty. I had to *know*. After the first operation I had been able to say with confidence, 'Now the problem is all over. Everything is permanently behind me!' but I couldn't necessarily do that this time. My whole way of thinking needed to be readjusted. But how was I going to accept even a small measure of uncertainty without letting the matter constantly irritate and unnerve me?

After lunch I lay down on the settee and looked at 'Mhairi's psalm' again:

> But I have calmed and quieted my soul,
> like a child quieted at its mother's breast.

The simple word-picture helped for a while but then the fear flooded back, fierce and insistent, and much too strong. It was then I knew I must seek particular help. The physical problem and its implications had grown so prominent in my thinking that it was now becoming impossible to gain relief. This new distress had brought me to a crisis point, perhaps even a turning?

Les was tired when he reached home at 7.30 p.m.

'There's always plenty of action in the control room at the start of the week,' he told me.

After making his late supper I sat down beside him on the settee and briefly explained what the doctor had said. Les sensed my deep-down apprehension.

'I'm sorry,' he said quietly.

'Well, I've appreciated knowing the facts. And those other areas of tissue could well have been innocent.'

'Maybe.'

The evening's broadcast promenade concert was starting and we sat and listened in silence to Tchaikovsky's violin concerto. Such haunting, expressive music! It helped to quieten my mind. Later, as the final movement

ended I tried to share my thoughts with Les but it was
hard.

'Sometimes it hurts so much, yet I can't really put the
feeling into words.'

'I know . . .'

It was a calm, exquisite evening. The livingroom windows framed a brilliant sky, aglow with bands of gold
and red.

'Maybe it would help if you talked things over with
Helen?' Les suggested. 'I could phone her now?' I hesitated, unwilling to interrupt her evening, but Les was
determined to follow through on his plan. 'She can
always say "no" if she's busy.'

'Yes, do drive over!' Helen invited as soon as Les
explained. 'We've been picking wild raspberries all
afternoon and now I'm simmering a pan of jam, so
Elaine can keep me company while I stir.'

Helen's welcome meant so much to me that evening. I
sat there on a stool in her homely kitchen and valued
being able to pour out the long accumulation of fear and
sadness. Helen understood. She had probably heard a
similar outpouring many times before. Then she introduced the need to accept, rather than constantly dismiss,
the facts of my situation. Her words underlined the
thoughts which had come to me over the weekend. All
along God had been bringing me to this point.

As we talked Helen helped me to recognize that, until
now, I had hankered for a complete release from the
medical problem, categorically rejecting any alternative.
But such an insistence was unreasonable and unworkable,
resulting in the growing inward uneasiness which was
evidenced by 'a need to go through with something'.

The crisis of acceptance was that 'something'. But I
could not go through with it alone. Everything within
me baulked at such an acquiescence. Only with Jesus'
strong help could I fully face the thought of an alternative (recurrence of the illness, even death), however
slight, in my case, the likelihood of such a development
might be. And only after such a facing and resultant
acceptance would I have something clearcut to hand

over to God: 'Lord, it is all yours. My health or a return
of the illness, or even my going, through death, to be
with you. Help me to rest it with you at last, acknow-
ledging your full wise control over my circumstances.'
These were the words I needed to bring to God, for only
after such a handing over would I be able to move on
beyond the present impasse to a new, more settled calm.
To firm hope.

I could see all this with my mind and it beckoned me
to clearcut action, but first I wanted to consider the
'death' aspect in more detail, for I was at that point
where all previous theoretical belief about 'being eternally safe in Jesus' now had to be tested out in a real-life
situation. I knew I must come to believe this truth not
merely with the easy assent of my mind but also with the
more exacting commitment of my heart. Only then could
it transform my whole attitude towards death, only then
could the sinister dread be effectively overcome.

Could I *really* rest back in the certainty that 'neither
death, nor life . . . nor things present, nor things to
come . . . will be able to separate us from the love of God
in Christ Jesus our Lord' (Rom 8:38–39)? Was I willing
to make these words a firm heart conviction so opening
myself to genuine peace, despite all else?

But my present life seemed so dear, so immediate, so
important. I could not bear for it to slip through my
hands and fade, moving on towards an inexorable end.
For all my mental belief in the joy of eternal life, instinct
demanded that I fight the wretched intrusion of death.
Death had never been 'natural'. It was an enemy.

Yet now I had begun to understand that, for all my
resistance, death would have to be faced sooner or later.
Enemy though it was, it must come to all living things.
And so what mattered much more than any instinctive
fighting was the firm affirmation that, as a result of
committing myself fully to Jesus and entering into the
inseparable bond with him which his own suffering made
possible, I was completely safe whether my body lived
on for many more years, or whether it grew weak and
died. I was his and he was mine. No one, no circumstance

whatever, could take me from him. And because he
lived eternally I would live eternally also. There would
always be an understandable fear of the actual dying
process, but death itself no longer possessed final power
over me. It had become no more than the means by
which I could be led on into indescribable joy!

I knew I must cling firmly to the strong comfort of
this truth even if there were yet to be hard, baffling
times ahead. Only then would I be more able to accept
health or suffering, physical strength or pain as coming
to me through the wise permission of Jesus who, with his
life so closely bound to mine, constantly worked for
nothing less than my highest good. Surely I could rest
back in this all-encompassing truth? And what great
cause for praise too, that every circumstance of my life
should be so designed to make me the more one with
Jesus who was 'all joy'!

All these different thoughts began when Helen showed
how essential acceptance was to the healing of a distressed
heart and mind.

'Yes, I can see the need for a definite act of acceptance
and heart commitment, but I'm not quite sure how to go
about it,' I admitted to Helen, just before we left for
home. 'Could you and some of the others show me?
Could you lay hands on me and pray, giving the whole
matter over to God, so I can find the relief I'm needing
so much?'

Helen was eager to take up the suggestion. 'I've been
wanting to help you in this way,' she said. 'Shall we ask
the members of the prayer group to come round to your
house on Wednesday evening?'

I felt grateful for Helen's immediate response to my
request, and as we drove home in the shadowed twilight
I felt much more at peace. I had already begun to share
the load which had become so heavy for me, and as a
result something definite was going to be done. Surely it
would mark a turning point?

A couple of evenings later eleven friends joined us in
the livingroom and this practical evidence of their concern and support further encouraged me. Long shafts

of sunlight had begun to slant down through the beeches on the far river bank—I could see the scene through the open back door—as Helen explained my difficulties with acceptance and subsequent request for help. Afterwards everyone gathered round, placing a hand on my head or shoulders, while Helen prayed, and I drew strong comfort from such a closeness. Comfort too as, by prayer, they took the burden of fear and sorrow, lifting its long-felt weight away so that I might start to know the relief of acceptance instead. In her simple prayer of committal, Helen made a clear request for healing, followed by an acknowledgement of God's sovereign right to say 'yes' or 'no' to our asking. Afterwards, still gathered in a circle, we sang, 'Praise God from whom all blessings flow . . .'

What an immediate upsurge of joy! It came flooding in where all the wretched apprehension had once been. There was a strong, evocative fragrance in the room too. Someone must have been wearing an expensive perfume and its beauty reminded me of Mary of Bethany's poured out ointment, given with such gladness. In the solemn joy of those few moments I felt a single tear slipping down my cheek and wondered if it was going to fall on someone's hand. But I need not feel embarrassed. They would understand. Nothing could lessen the delight of our oneness with each other in the healing love of Jesus.

Much later that night, when the house was still and Les asleep, I lay looking out at the dark sky, seeing the first piercing star. That night I *did* feel 'calmed and quieted . . . like a child at its mother's breast'. Fear and its accompanying depression had been countered at last, their long-standing grip undermined. Acceptance had begun to take their place and so there could be quiet and calm, at least for the present. The matter had been rested in God's hands. He would wisely keep and order all I could not yet know. And so I was safe.

A phrase from the book *Blessings** went through my mind: '. . . suffering can teach ordinary people some extraordinary things.' Perhaps this was starting to happen, even in my own experience?

* Mary Craig *Blessings* (Hodder & Stoughton 1979). By permission.

8

'He Kens It A'!'

The magnificent, unusually hot summer was slowly ending but there was still time to fit in a short break before the colder weather set in. And a caravan holiday had been one of my important goals. Ian, our minister, knew this and towards the end of August kindly towed his caravan across to a Deeside site so Les and I could have a few days away on our own. All the previous week I enjoyed making preparations and at the same time tried to remember everything the lads would need at home. They were very excited at the thought of being left to themselves for a few days and kept asking when we were going, how long we'd be away, and what time of day we planned to return.

In between baking and shopping I used the time resting upstairs to write two articles for a magazine. They had not been requested but I prepared them partly as a stimulus for my still dull mind, and partly because I longed to be busy with writing again. The task took much longer than usual and I had to make several drafts of each short piece before they were finally ready for the post. If nothing else, the exercise had shown how inefficient my thinking had become, which was disturbing as well as frustrating.

But the frustration was forgotten in the pleasure of our holidaymaking. We were both 'green' to caravanning, but quickly discovered the unique pleasure to be gained from such compact living. Not that much time was spent

in the caravan, for warm clear sunshine welcomed us
each morning and we could hardly wait to set off and
explore the grandeur of our highland surroundings.
One day we drove along a narrow birch-lined lane to the
Forest of Birse, and came across a small chapel close to a
tumbling burn. We paused in its cool stillness for a while
and then walked along beside the sparkling water. All of
a sudden a snake appeared on the pathway, slithering
between us, and we stopped in silent fascination to watch
as it wove its way slowly in and out of nearby rocks and
vanished.

'Must have been a viper,' Les said. 'The V-marking on
its head was clearly visible, wasn't it?'

On another day we drove along the Dee, then continued west from Braemar, up Glenshee and across the
hills to visit Les's aunt in Pitlochry. Pink rosebay willowherb lined many of the Perthshire lanes, but the grassy
roadside banks were also dusty and brown after the
summer's heat and roaming sheep impatiently jostled
one another for shade in the wide dry ditches. It was late
when we returned to the caravan in the calm glow of a
lingering sunset. By then the steep scree-slopes of the
mountains were patterned with long shadows and the
Royal Standard was hanging motionless above the tower
of Balmoral Castle.

I had always wanted to drive over the summit of the
well-known Cairn O' Mount so we chose this route on
our last day and were amazed by so wide and wild a view
of craggy mountains and empty moors.

'What a place!' I exclaimed, revelling in its remoteness.
'I'd just love to live up here amid all this magnificent
solitude.'

'No you wouldn't,' Les objected. 'You'd soon get
bored!'

On our way back, close to the village of Strachan, we
stopped to explore a steep woodland track I'd noted in
the morning. An evening paper lay propped between
two large stones at the foot of the path and soon after we
started climbing, footsteps approached from the road
below. A woodcutter passed, paper in hand, and smiled

in greeting. At the brow of the hill we came across his
old trailer, set beside a rough wooden shack. A thin grey
cat leapt out of the gold-tinted bracken, offered us a
quick glance, then bounded up the trailer steps to join
her master for supper, and before long we smelled para-
ffin on the warm air. It was an unexpected scene there
beneath the tall straight pines and slanting sunlight, and
I couldn't help wondering how long the woodcutter had
lived there, alone in the silent forest.

That night early-autumn rain fell, a gentle whispered
sound on the caravan roof. It was still damp when Ian
and Mary arrived next morning to tow the caravan back,
thoughtfully bringing a flask of coffee and some home-
made biscuits to share with us.

'How about doing this again?' Ian suggested, as we all
sat around the small table.

'Well, if the caravan is free sometime we'd love to!' I
told him, and wondered if he'd guessed that the reaching of this holiday goal had brought us special happiness.

All was well when we reached home. The boys had
obviously had a quick dash-round with the vacuum
cleaner before our arrival and Miss Puss was looking
round and content, much overfed. Before long Rachel
walked in, home for the weekend, and we decided to
make a large salad for lunch using some of the lettuces
which were now crowding the vegetable patch.

'Let's have some radishes too!' I suggested, so Rachel
went out to fetch a few and was gone for quite a while,
eventually returning with a small bunch which she started
to wash and slice.

'They seem very tough. Rather an odd colour too,' I
heard her mutter and, glancing round, I saw she was
trying to chop up half a dozen very immature beetroots,
much-prized survivors from a whole packet of seed.
There were now only four or five left along the row
outside. But still enough, perhaps, for one jar of beetroot
chutney? 'Sorry Mum, I must have made a mistake!'
Rachel confessed, and I forced myself to laugh. 'Rachel's
radishes' became a teasing point for the rest of the
weekend.

*   *   *

Autumn was steadily creeping in. Both sycamores on the
nearside river bank were heavy with seed keys and during
the last week of August I heard the robin's clear post-
summer song. A song of beauty, yet touched with sadness
too. Summer was all but over.

Somehow a sense of sorrow and regret began to seep
into my mind too. It came from beyond myself this time,
'a sadness growing' in the world around and reaching
out to me as well. It was not the distressing sadness of
non-acceptance, but rather the quiet poignant sorrow of
acquiescence. The realization that, for all the relief of
resting a hard matter with God, there would yet be
anguish to be faced. Such was the inevitable mosaic of
this here-and-now life, where pain and joy must always
mingle, inseparable. I began to understand that such a
sorrow—the same sorrow of acquiescence which Jesus
had known before his suffering— far from being a matter for shame, was rather the setting within which he
waited to identify himself with me still more, offering
even greater solace.

This reassurance considerably eased the pain of my
sorrow and one afternoon, when Les and I were sitting
out on the back doorstep, I attempted to describe its
newly-discovered meaning, but it was hard for him to
understand. So we eventually fell silent, enjoying the
sleepy stillness of our September surroundings. All of a
sudden Les said, 'Did you hear that strange noise?'

'No, what was it like?'

'A kind of pop. I'm sure some of the pods on the
broom brushes are splitting open. Listen again . . .'

I held my breath, straining for the sound, but could
only hear the river's murmur and the faint cries of two
gulls circling high up in the pale sky. There was a som-
breness about approaching autumn, but we were soon to
discover its own rich beauty too.

Once the new school term began and the family dispersed, I decided to start on a postponed programme of
blanket washing and cupboard cleaning. But before long

the weariness unexpectedly returned, forcing me to rest
for several hours each day. I found this interruption of
household plans irritating, particularly after the physical
boost gained from our holiday. Then too, loss of appetite
and accompanying nausea became much more marked
when the weariness increased. Before long I started to
become entangled in the problem again. It plagued my
thinking and prolonged the weariness, so that I began to
think of myself as still being ill. Determined to break
free from this downward spiral, I would get up from
resting and busy myself around the house, ironing a pile
of laundry or trying out a new recipe for supper, but if
Les caught me at it he'd immediately object.

'Now what are you doing?' he'd say in a despairing
way.

'Just trying to get on top of my problem.'

'You'll never lick it like that. You need more rest, not
less.'

Then he would urge me to lie down on the settee once
more, hovering until I did so.

I supposed he must be right for resting did eventually
restore a measure of strength, but I knew I must also
guard against getting into a rut of resting on occasions
when I needed to be up and doing. It would be easy,
after a long illness, to give in rather than constantly, yet
carefully, move back towards normality. This was where
legitimate 'fighting' came in, in order to extend the
record of achievement. Goals were a part of this progression too, offering all-important incentive. I realized
my need for a new set of goals now that I had achieved
the Summer Lunch in June, Catherine's wedding in
July, and the holiday in August. What could my new
goals be? I decided to plan a short visit down to my
sister, Wendy, in Dorset as compensation for cancelling
because of illness earlier in the year. Then there were
two invitations for speaking engagements in October
too. Yes, all of these could be my immediate goals, off-
setting the irksomeness of any lingering physical limitations. Then, as well, I determined not to overlook points
of particular progress. The dull aching in my side had

all but gone and I definitely looked better. Friends frequently encouraged me by commenting on this.

It seemed a shocking admission, but sometimes I regretted the fact that soon I would no longer receive the
particular sympathy of others. The circumstances which
had brought their thoughtful visits, cards, letters and
gifts might have been unwelcome, but being in the focus
of attention had offered unexpected pleasure. I had
enjoyed the concern and now regretted its inevitable
fading. As a result it was tempting to invite ongoing
sympathy by wearing a tired look and answering a friend's
enquiries with, 'Yes, I am making progress, but . . .' then
listing complaints. Not enlarging upon them (to have
done so would have resulted in a lessening of sympathy)
but sharing enough to evoke continuing concern. I knew I
had sometimes fallen into this trap. It was one side of a
peculiar contradiction which pulled me back and forth
in opposing directions. The genuine yearning to be
strong and well again was being constantly challenged
by a hankering for sympathy. Did others experience
such a tension? I wondered. I had never heard anyone
speak about it. How did they overcome it? I concluded
that the resolving would come in time. As strength returned I would become convinced of renewed health (I
was not yet fully convinced, almost expecting the periods
of weariness) and then I would despise any such seeking
after sympathy.

During those low times of weakness I discovered again
how important it was deliberately to keep open to fun
and laughter. The family gave me plenty of scope for
this. So did the cat. One Friday afternoon I found her
sunning herself on the garden seat, sitting very prim
and proper but with her black face completely veiled in
a close-weave cobweb, scattered with fluff and leaf scraps.
How ridiculous she looked! The more so as she sat
blinking slowly and steadily at me, contemptuous of my
amusement. Minutes later Rachel and Stuart burst in at
the front door, just home on the afternoon bus. Stuart
was hot with indignation.

'Rachel's run out of money again. She even borrowed

her bus fare from me!' he blurted out, as he glared at
her over the rim of a large glass of juice.

'But guess what,' Rachel hastily countered. 'I came
across quite a stash of cash earlier this week. Wasn't that
great!'

'Where did you find it?' I asked, suspicious.

'Under a flowerpot in my room. One pound fifty
altogether. Enough for the next two dinners!'

Les, just in from work, rolled his eyes upwards in
mock despair, 'Daughters!' And I smiled to myself as I
spread the cheese and tomato topping over a large pizza
for the family. Friday nights always offered a volatile
mixture of anger and fun, companionship and rivalry.
You never knew which turn things would take next. It
was intriguing to stand on the sidelines and watch.
Therapeutic too.

Next morning the postman brought my large self-
addressed envelope, returned from the magazine editor.
It was heavy and fat, and I didn't need to open it to
know both articles had been rejected. After glancing
through them again I recognized how dull they were
and this triggered concern about future writing projects,
particularly work on a Christmas piece requested by an
editor in London. He didn't realize how slow and
laboured my writing had now become, adversely affect-
ing the end result. The problem nagged at my mind as I
prepared weekend meals that morning. Should I turn
down the request, explaining I was unable to write at
present? No, my mind needed the discipline of working
towards writing goals. Besides, a negative response could
jeopardize future contacts with the editor. In the end I
decided to draft the article the following week and then,
later on, to ask Les for criticism of the developing manuscript. His help in this way had so often proved invaluable.

I remembered that the following week was going to be
full in other ways too. We were expecting close friends,
Christopher and Charlotte, to join us for a few days and
the thought of their coming brought much pleasure. I
enjoyed offering hospitality and had found it hard to be
often prevented from doing so during recent months.

The Thompsons were easy guests, too, always eager to fit in with family routine rather than be entertained.

Their visit was as happy as any of the previous times we had spent together. At least, until the last afternoon. Earlier in the week we went for short walks up into the pine forests or along the river bank towards the 'Shakkin' Briggie', but then the weather broke, shrouding our surroundings in cold damp mist.

'Now we're definitely in Scotland!' Christopher joked.

From then on we spent much of our time talking around the fireside. There was so much mutual catching-up to do! And I appreciated hearing all about their work, church activities, and future plans. Our time together was going by much too fast.

Heavy rain began to fall on our last day together, and large drops dribbled down the windows, leaving wide dusty trails.

'Another fireside afternoon!' Charlotte decided, with a smile. 'But I'm glad of a chance to sit still and do nothing. Life's much too busy most of the time!'

As we chatted on, Christopher began to question me about my illness, the subject being of interest to him after medical experience abroad, including several encounters with this particular condition. 'It's rare in Britain,' he told me, 'but fairly common in certain tropical countries, particularly amongst beer-drinking men!'

Intrigued, I began to draw more on Christopher's knowledge and he seemed happy to answer my questions.

'Of course, the problem never spreads to other parts of the body, does it?' I tentatively asked at one point, waiting for him to say, 'No, it's always localized.' (Despite my overall acceptance this fear still frequently stabbed at my mind, demanding repeated reassurance.)

Christopher paused. 'Well, it doesn't spread above the diaphragm,' he answered slowly.

I began to feel uneasy. Was his answer an evasion? Had I put him in a difficult position? It seemed best quickly to change the subject for I couldn't bring myself to ask the question which was already forming in my mind, 'Can it spread below the diaphragm then?'

*   *   *

Christopher and Charlotte left early next morning,
about the time Les set off for his weekend day-shift. In
the afternoon I walked alone along the river bank, sudden strong gusts of wind tugging at my headscarf. A
golden labrador was swimming back and forth across
the cold tumble of water, panting loudly, proud of his
achievement. Then a large fish leapt, silver in the sunlight. There was no sign of the dippers. I stood by the
graceful birches and listened to each mingled sound: the
rush of water, the roar of the wind tearing at the beech
trees in the far woods, the rustle of dry broom pods,
soon to hang empty and misshapen on hardening stems.
Then I walked upstream beyond the wide bend where
the water, unhindered by rocks, flowed on in silence.
Thistle heads were bursting with silken down and each
rosehip was a swollen, gleaming scarlet. The wind had
teased clouds of soft seeds from the banks of rosebay
willowherb and the air was full of their drifting. I heard
the urgent flap of wings as a frightened moorhen darted
across to the far bank, then saw a single golden beech
leaf fall to meet the dark water. Autumn was so full of
solemn beauty!

My mind, free of the week's busy, ordinary thoughts,
was suddenly vulnerable to the onslaught of apprehension which Christopher's half-answer had triggered.
What had he meant? His words kept tracking back and
forth across my mind, testing out the genuineness of my
earlier commitment to God, and arousing the all-but-
forgotten anguish of 'not knowing'. This time I knew I
could not share my thoughts with Anne or Helen. There
was a limit to the amount of outpouring a person could
inflict on even the closest of friends. Nor did I feel able
to express my feelings to Les. He was so close to me and
doing so would only sadden him.

A post-operative check was due the following afternoon so I decided to take this opportunity to question
the surgeon further, confident he would supply all the
reassurance I needed. But would he mind my asking?

And would he have time in the midst of a busy clinic?

It was 'dreich' and grey next day, and large old leaves were pressed down against the wet city pavements, crushed by hurrying footsteps. I sat in one of the clinic cubicles looking out through the grimy window to a single sycamore standing close against the building, still clutching at its dying leaves and heavy seed-keys. Footsteps approached. A different doctor walked in. A complete stranger. He was quick and friendly with his greeting, quick with the examination, quick with his one comment, 'Everything is going well, isn't it!'

How could I reply? What could I say? My carefully memorized questions seemed suddenly inappropriate and I was swamped by bewildered disappointment.

'There's still a small amount of pain, but it's much better than before . . .' my voice trailed off. 'I still find eating difficult because of the nausea but I'll keep working at it . . .'

I so much wanted to ask if the outlook really was good, if so small a growth definitely wouldn't spread, but forced the questions back. The surgeon was too busy. Perhaps he'd think I was being unnecessarily pessimistic and brush my anxiety aside with a quick, 'Oh, I shouldn't worry about that!' and I'd feel foolish.

The surgeon picked up the pile of notes and opened the door.

'We'll see you again in three months' time. No need to worry. We've got rid of all those nasty lumps now.'

Then he was gone, leaving me unconvinced. The tears spilled over as I pulled on the peach-coloured skirt Rachel had made. There had been no chance to share my questions, no opportunity for the specific reassurance I had counted on so much. Only his mention of 'all those nasty lumps', leaving my mind more turmoiled still.

As I walked out into the damp misty street I decided to counter the disappointment with a deliberate change of plan, knowing I must offset the problem by turning thoughts outwards. Maybe by visiting someone? Isobel? I had been intending to call on this city friend for several weeks, ever since hearing her husband had left her. I drove straight to Isobel's bungalow and settled gratefully down beside her warm fireside.

'Let me make you some tea,' Isobel offered, and I wondered if she'd noticed the sadness and anxiety on my face. It helped to sit in silence and listen as Isobel quite spontaneously expressed some of the deep sorrow with which she'd been struggling over many months. I felt myself reaching out more and more towards her, able to feel another person's pain in a way not possible before. Tears came to Isobel's eyes and I longed to say, 'Don't feel embarrassed. Tears come to my eyes sometimes too,' but I remained silent, listening and listening, trying to bring her a measure of comfort by taking some of the pain into myself.

The afternoon was fading, and soon Isobel's three lively little girls scampered in from school. We walked down the stone steps of the porch and out onto the pavement together.

'I think God is going to give me a visitor every day this week!' Isobel said quietly, and I saw her face break into a quick, expectant smile. Then, 'Take care of yourself, won't you?' she urged, looking at me with sudden concern.

She waited in the doorway as I drove off up the hill. Dear Isobel. It had been so right that I should visit her that afternoon. Perhaps we would never come so close to one another as when we stooped to bind up each other's hurts and wounds.

I took the main road route through the busy streets, then out up the long hill as evening sunlight was breaking free from the heavy clouds to fill the whole wide valley with slanting gold. Why had I been so tense and anxious all day? So set on seeking reassurance yet again? Had I not committed it all, present and future, to Jesus? Would he not wisely keep and order all I could not yet know? It was the same sequence all over again. A small seed of fear, so soon grown to threatening proportions.

Although fear no longer held my mind in a tight underlying grip, it had nonetheless crept back following Christopher's words and I knew I must therefore the more affirm my earlier commitment lest fear gain an increasing foothold. Its reappearance had come as a very real test of 'resting the matter' with God, and I sensed he had permitted this testing-point simply so that I might discover the strength of depending upon him the more. All these different thoughts went through my mind as I drove down into the valley and across towards Bennachie in the west, the sun's rays now low and penetrating, streaming from the hills ahead. I knew I must return to take refuge in Jesus, letting him be to me even more than I had expected from the surgeon—reassurance, comfort, calm.

'Lord, I want to rest,' I found myself asking. 'Take me as I am this afternoon, all "trachled" and sad. I lean back against your strong, sheltering protection, your complete goodness and control . . .'

I was aware that, in my frailty, I would need to reaffirm my acceptance of circumstances and return to a place of rest again and again. Yet there was no need to resent the repetition if, through it, restfulness became a more frequent experience. Each relearning would take me on further than before. Wasn't all of life a progression towards an eventual arrival, every stage a part of the final completion?

Once home I began to feel very weary, physically spent. Les insisted on my lying down all evening. 'How about a day in bed tomorrow too?' he urged. For once I didn't resist, aware of my need for recreative quiet and rest.

* * *

During the morning of my 'rest day' Hazel called in and stayed for a couple of hours. I enjoyed young Fiona's lively chatter and in between playing with bricks and drawing pictures for her, Hazel and I had time to talk. She told me about the early days of her marriage spent far out in the countryside where 'you could look up at night and see the stars and think of God'. Then she shared the difficulties of being often left on her own now to care for a large family while her husband worked off-shore on a North Sea oil rig.

'But I've got it easy compared to some,' Hazel added, going on to say how bewildered she often felt by all the suffering in the world. Fiona interrupted, wanting her mother to help with a jigsaw puzzle, but Hazel was still deep in thought as she fitted the large wooden pieces awkwardly together.

'Somehow I think God wants to use the hard times to bring us to him, if we'll come . . .' she began, but before she could explore the idea further Fiona tugged at her sleeve.

'Mum, you've put those pieces in wrong!'

It was almost midday and, as Hazel stood up to go, I reminded her of the yellow and white carnations she had given me all those weeks ago, telling her again of how they had brought me closer to God.

'Och, but they were so small a gift!' she objected.

'No they weren't. I'll never forget how much they meant that day!'

The lunchbreak siren sounded out across the fields from the nearby granite quarry and Fiona pulled insistently at her mother's hand. 'Come awa' hame, Mum!'

Hazel paused, then bent to kiss me before leaving. How much I appreciated this unexpected expression of her friendship, aware that local friends rarely demonstrated their affection in such a way. Doing so was special. And amid my appreciation for Hazel's thoughtful touch I realized that so many friendships, ordinary before, now possessed new depth and meaning. It was another aspect of the unexpected richness to be found even in the midst of suffering.

It was helpful to lie back and rest all afternoon, to listen to music and absorb the surrounding beauty, so that I might be reassured deep down where there was still a hunger for order and meaning and certainty. And while resting in the quiet bedroom one or two ideas for the magazine article began to develop in my mind. I scribbled them down on a scrap of paper, glad to have made a tentative start.

Over the following week, with much crossing out and

rephrasing, the piece took shape. When it was in a read-
able form Les gave constructive criticism and eventually,
after another typing, the article was ready for posting. I
had completed it on our wedding anniversary and, after
happily dropping the envelope into the village pillar
box, Les took me out into the country for a drive and
lunch at a Deeside hotel. It was quiet and beautiful
there, an ideal setting. My appetite soon picked up at the
sight of the menu and we ate our way through melon,
roast beef and ice cream sundaes while, just beyond the
wide windows, the Dee flowed on, smooth and shining.
Coffee was served in the high-ceilinged, chintz-furnished
lounge and, with the whole room to ourselves, we sat in
silence to watch black and white migrant ducks preening
on the further bank of the river, and an occasional
salmon rising. What a specially glad occasion! Later Les
and I strolled along beside the water and then, before
driving away, stopped to share the day's reading from
Living Light. Its exultant affirmation could not have been
more appropriate: 'God has given you all of the present
and all of the future. All are yours, and you belong to
Christ, and Christ is God's' (1 Cor 3:22–23 The Living
Bible). Les read the words, then turned to me. 'We
certainly couldn't ask for more than that, could we?'
And I caught the look of quiet joy in his eyes.

He insisted on buying me a bouquet of yellow crysanthemums as we made our way home and, just outside
the village, we stopped to cut five tall roadside ferns to
go with the flowers. Later I arranged them in a glass jug
beside the fireplace. A final perfect touch to our day!
Life was full of offered joy, but I had to want to be made
willing to step on beyond my difficulties before I could
begin to delight in such richness. The initial 'wanting to
be made willing' was essential but far from easy, especially at low times and, though I could not have known it
amid the pleasure of our day, there were to be a few
more such 'lows'.

Nonetheless, for a while the happiness of our anniversary celebration and an awareness of gradual improvement kept me on the upswing and, when Les was off-

duty, we were able to get out and about more, as well as spend time on shared household tasks. One of these, as September ended, was the last harvesting of vegetables from our small garden plot, including what was left of the beetroot. Seven small beets in all. Les boiled and peeled them while I minced up some cooking apples and then we simmered the two together, adding vinegar, sugar and seasoning, to make a couple of jars of chutney.

'It will go well with winter salads,' I told Les. He nodded. 'Yes, for just one or two! And next season we won't send Rachel out to pick radishes!'

That same week I reached a smaller, more mundane goal—a shopping expedition to restock at one of the large city supermarkets. Les helped and as we came home later, after a picnic lunch, I felt particularly pleased and satisfied, even if rather tired. An hour's rest soon restored my energy and afterwards I set off up the road to leave some strawberry jam and a bag of plums on a friend's back doorstep. Her husband had been out of work for over two years and we felt very much for them. The gift seemed rather small and insignificant as I set the items down by the door, but it was important not to forget their need now that our own unemployment difficulties were over.

Afterwards I drove a little further on, wanting to spend time with an elderly friend whose company I always enjoyed. I found Miss Emily returning from a slow walk to the village bridge and back.

'I'm awfu' pleased I didnae miss ye! There's somebody up above has got his han' on us!' she told me, taking my arm. She seemed rather weak (perhaps feeling her ninety-plus years now?) and complained of back pain as we made our way towards her front door.

'A few days ago I was feeling awfu' sad and sair,' Miss Emily went on, stopping all of a sudden to gaze up into my face. 'But then I stood and lookit out o' the window at a' the fields and hills. God *is* there. He kens it a', I thocht tae mysel'. And he dis. He dis!'

We went indoors and chatted for a while, Miss Emily reaching far back in her mind to childhood events which she remembered as clearly as if they'd happened that very week.

'Sometimes—just once a year—we bairns would climb Bennachie. Right to the top! And even though I was much sma'er than my brithers, I'd struggle along ahint wi' a piece in my pooch and heather richt up tae my knees . . .'

I loved listening, trying to pick up as much as possible despite Miss Emily's marked local dialect. Once or twice I missed a few phrases and, quick as ever, she stopped mid-sentence and confronted me. 'Ye didnae understan', did ye?'

'Not *every* word,' I confessed.

'Well I'll speak slower then,' she decided, and I felt uncomfortably aware of my English ignorance.

When her grand old sideboard clock chimed five I suddenly remembered I needed to cook the spaghetti sauce for tea, so jumped up. 'I'll have to go!'

Miss Emily frowned disapprovingly at the interruption, then reached out her small thin hand to mine.

'Must ye gang awa'? But wait, I'll come wi' ye!' And she insisted on accompanying me back to the car despite the gathering grey clouds and chill wind. Dear Miss Emily. She little knew how much she had cheered me.

*　　*　　*

It was a week or two later that I began to grow very weary and sick, then discouraged too. Les was on day-shift and, alone in the house one afternoon, I sat by the fire and tried to forget myself by concentrating on a few favourite New Testament verses from 1 Corinthians, and a time of prayer for various friends who were facing much greater difficulties. But the plan didn't work. Instead I kept thinking, 'What would those who've been praying say if they knew how low I was today?' I recalled that calm summer's evening when Helen had asked God for healing, but forgot her acknowledgement of his right to say 'yes' or 'no' to her request. Instead I worried myself with the thought that these recurrent bouts of

illness must indicate I was not trusting God enough for
the immediate healing he was waiting to give.

Guilt feelings grew large in my mind. 'If I had genuinely expected Jesus to remove the illness I wouldn't be
like this now.' It was an inevitable tangle, reached because
I was refusing to consider anything other than an outright healing as being honouring to God. 'Absolute
physical healing must be God's will for us,' I'd decided.
'And so absence of such a clearcut healing must indicate
failure on my part to co-operate with that will.'

As I allowed my mind to linger on such rigid and
innaccurate reasoning the guilt feelings intensified and I
concluded I was letting God down by continuing in
physical weakness and its associated discouragement.
This led me to resent lingering illness the more, and to
despise myself for being dragged down by its irksome
weight.

I had overlooked one vital fact, illustrated in the Bible
and indicated in many of its promises, particularly Jesus'
words, 'And I will do whatever you ask for in my name,
so that the Father's glory will be shown' (Jn 14:13 GNB).

It was important to remember that all the circumstances
God allowed in my life were designed primarily to bring
him glory, and though I might consider that outright
healing would glorify him most, his viewpoint could be
quite the reverse. I needed to be equally open and receptive to such an alternative for surely, as the conclusion
of the New Testament 'faith chapter', Hebrews 11, so
clearly showed, God gave faith *to suffer and die* as well as
faith to be delivered. And ultimately either alternative
brought God increased glory, inexplicable though that
might be to a human mind. It was a strong, compelling
truth, able to take me far on beyond the frustrations of
my own faulty reasoning.

But, for the time being, I had no eyes for such a truth.
Instead I was stuck with exaggerated feelings of guilt,
and before long my thoughts went back to the friends
who had gathered with Helen to pray that August evening. Had they been observing me even more closely
since, eager for evidence of healing and personal victory

over circumstances? Had I disappointed them, even as I
felt I had disappointed God? The likelihood of their
having looked to me in vain for such an example not
only increased my remorse, but also pressed hard against
a tender inner spot. I was not projecting the success
image with which I so much wanted to impress those
who'd faithfully prayed over the months. And now, because I had let them down, they were sure to think less
of me . . .

Just when I was becoming tangled up in all this hurt
pride and self-accusation Anne arrived. I wondered if
she had some inkling of my confusion for, as soon as she
had settled into the armchair opposite she asked, 'Do
you mind if I share a Bible verse? It's something the
Lord showed me today when I was thinking about you.'

She had brought her own New International Version
and read to me from it: 'And the God of all grace, who
called you to his eternal glory in Christ, after you have
suffered a little while, will himself restore and make you
strong, firm and steadfast. To him be the power for ever
and ever' (1 Pet 5:10).

Anne waited for a few moments, then looked straight
across to me. 'The Lord will completely restore you! I'm
sure of it!' she insisted, eager that I, too, should enter
fully into her new confidence. I hesitated, immediately
on the defensive because of my mood, and not knowing
how to respond, not even knowing if I wanted to appreciate her verse at present. My mind went back to the
few occasions when I'd tried to share an appropriate
verse with Les during his difficulties, so sure he'd be
much helped. But he had only looked away, his eyes sad.
Now I could understand. But nonetheless I didn't want
to crush Anne's confidence.

'The Lord is already restoring me,' I said evasively,
and then we sat in silence for a few moments before
going on to talk about other things.

Later, when Anne had left, I reconsidered her clearcut
insistence, 'The Lord will completely restore you!' *Was*
this the way God had chosen to bring glory to himself in
my life even if, as the verse with its 'suffered a while'

indicated, it was to be a gradual rather than immediate healing? The possibility intrigued me. Perhaps God had given Anne this specific understanding of his purpose in my circumstances, an 'inner knowing' much as I had experienced in another context earlier in the year? At any other time the fact of his giving Anne such an insight would have immediately excited and encouraged me, but it wasn't like that on this particular afternoon. I wasn't ready to be 'completely restored' yet. Instead I wanted to continue in the aftermath of illness for just a little longer so there might yet be opportunity to prove I could be brave and buoyant in the midst of a difficulty, not afterwards when cheerfulness was easy. I still wanted to impress those around me. It was a raw admission, but it was the truth.

But at the same time there was a reverse side to the matter. When I could forget my reputation with others and look at circumstances simply from my own point of view I longed to be completely well and free, both in my body and in my thinking. Deep down I recognized the pride behind the 'success image' I wanted to portray, and yearned to be released from the adverse circumstances out of which such an attitude had developed. On the one hand I didn't yet want to be well, but on the other hand I did. It was another facet of the same puzzling contradiction which had so often tugged me back and forth during this time of recovery; the benefit of renewed health was being challenged by the advantage still to be gained from continued weakness. An extraordinary position to be in! And impossible to understand until one had experienced it personally.

By now three months had passed since the second operation, and the first of the quarterly blood checks was almost due. I was aware that anticipation of this was a factor in my present weakness and longed for the test appointment to come and go. Apparently, if the malignancy ever recurred it would reveal itself by secreting raised levels of a certain protein into the bloodstream. 'So immediate detection would be possible,' our doctor had explained, 'making you much more fortunate than most people!' He was right of course, but the follow-up tests still appeared threatening, mostly because they were so new. In time, perhaps, I would become more relaxed, hardly noticing the passing weeks, even forgetting when the next test was due. Was that how it would all become, a small, insignificant matter? (I had been told that after about four years the frequency of testing would be reduced, but the need for it would continue quite far into the future due to the slow-growing nature of this particular lesion.)

I felt apprehensive as the day for the first test approached, though was careful to mask my feelings, smiling my way into the village health centre that morning as if nothing was up.

'The result will come through in about three weeks' time,' the nurse said, explaining details about the test procedure, and her understanding helped to reassure me. A weight check had to be done too. I'd lost three pounds.

'But I'll quickly regain them if I concentrate on high protein foods, won't I?' I asked. The nurse agreed and gave me some helpful diet tips, so I went home with several new ideas to implement.

'And you must also eat lots more glucose and Complan,' Les decided, after hearing about the weight loss. 'So you'll grow all fat and round like the cat!'

9

'Love Me for Myself Alone . . .'

October began with several cold damp days. Grey clouds hung low over the far hills, becoming ragged and frayed as they dragged against the upland fields, and high above, muted by the mist, we heard the first calls of the wild geese, flying south from their Icelandic breeding grounds. October was also the month I planned to visit Wendy in Dorset, and after this brief holiday (the jet flight both ways was a real treat) I returned feeling refreshed by the warm west country air and much more able to tackle the long winter ahead. By then autumn gales had struck and we watched the beech trees protesting in a tangled frenzy as the fierce wind clawed at their leafy branches. A few dandelion clocks and flowers were still holding their own on the grassy riverbank, but the rosebay willowherb by the water's edge was dying fast, its tall stems stiff and bedraggled, and every seed case spent.

The evenings were drawing in and the lads missed their frequent cycle rides to the Lord's Throat stretch of the Don and picnics at the large flat rock where, after a long swim, they had cooked sausages on an open fire.

'Life here at home is such a miserable bore!' Stuart complained one blustery Saturday afternoon as he flung himself down on the settee, letting his long body spill over at either end. It was Les's off-duty week so he challenged the three youngsters to a few rounds of badminton and, playing entirely with his left hand, soundly

158

thrashed Murray. Stuart was still disgruntled when they returned later for a griddle scone tea, but soon afterwards Rachel made us all bellow with laughter by constructing a set of false teeth for herself from thick strips of orange peel. How ridiculous she looked!

Some time the following week a small thin envelope arrived through our letterbox. An acceptance from the magazine editor! The article would be appearing in his Christmas issue. This brought immediate encouragement. Perhaps my dull mind was clearing at last? And the resulting boost in confidence helped as I prepared a couple of simple talks and set off for the planned speaking engagements that month. Les came with me to the second and we left early in order to enjoy a picnic lunch at one of the small fishing villages en route. We chose Sandend, arriving at high tide as angry waves were flinging themselves one upon another against the stone wall of the small harbour. Quite a dramatic sight to watch as we sat in the car and ate our salad sandwiches. Three redshanks kept darting back and forth across the narrow quay, and a cluster of turnstones flew down to forage amongst the old cans and rope ends on the strip of sandy beach.

Much later we drove home as long thin shadows were starting to reach out across upland fields. The leisurely car journey offered a welcome chance to think and talk, and my mind went back again to Anne's certainty of my healing.

'Do you think God has given her a specific "inner knowing"?' I asked Les, after telling him about our conversation and the verse Anne shared.

'He could have done.'

'Do you have the same inner certainty?'

Les considered the question for a few moments. 'No, I haven't, but that's not to say I'm not open to receiving it.'

His point about remaining open was important, emphasizing my own need to be receptive to whatever Jesus wanted to show me. We talked on about the matter for a while longer.

'Do you think prayer for healing needs to be preceded

by this definite inner certainty?' I asked.

'Yes, that would be true because, together with the inward conviction, God's Spirit also gives specific faith and expectancy in the matter. It's all bound up together surely? And then the completion comes when the healing is actually given, whether instantaneously or over a period of time.'

Les's clear reasoning helped to answer the questioning in my mind, and most of all showed what my own response to the situation should be. At present, in the absence of any personal inner certainty regarding healing, I myself should continue to rest the whole matter with Jesus, accepting whatever his purpose proved to be. Maybe, in time, he would give me an 'inner knowing' too, and with it a clearcut belief in his complete healing, confirming the conviction Anne had already expressed.

I felt myself relaxing as we drove on across the gentle hills towards Bennachie, which stood in sharp outline against the horizon, while all the spread of sky around turned to vivid red and gold. A twilight stillness had fallen on the village by the time we reached home, and in the semi-darkness we almost trampled on the letters scattered across the doormat. One was from the hospital out-patient department. They had made an appointment for a liver ultra-sound scan on November 2nd. 'Just a routine check,' I reminded Les, then to reassure myself, 'and it's bound to be fine!'

*　　　*　　　*

Winter was creeping in. Sharp slivers of ice began to blow across from the hills and each night fierce frosts gnawed at the last brave annuals along our garden border, blackening their colourful blooms, and finally leaving them limp and dead. The leaves were falling fast too, even on calm days, and as I watched them spin down onto the river bank I realized their breeze-blown freedom was over. From now on they would remain earthbound, soon to be crushed and forgotten. Flocks of pink-footed geese continued to fly south across the stormy sky, in

long V-shaped skeins. How I loved to listen to their
solemn calls, and also to the wing-beats of the arriving
swans. The first, quite alone, flew low over our house on
the last evening of October and we wondered if the
whooper which had lingered upriver all summer might
have joined it, for there was no sign of the lone swan
when we next drove along that winding Donside road.

When the day came for my liver scan Les drove me to
the hospital straight after breakfast. I was first on the list
that morning so there was no time to sit fighting off
apprehension.

A nurse helped me up onto the high couch and I
wondered if Rachel was somewhere around. She had
promised to look out for me that morning. The doctor
came in and sat down, then he moved the probe slowly
back and forth across my stomach, carefully studying
the complicated readings on the screen. I tried to gauge
what he was thinking but there was no give-away expression on his face. Surely everything would prove normal?
Surely there wouldn't be even the slightest evidence of a
recurrence? The radiologist switched off the machine.
Then he turned to face me.

'You can go now. It's all fine!'

Oh, what a tremendous relief! I pulled on my clothes
as fast as I could and hurried down the corridor to join
Les. By then Rachel was there too and I hardly needed
to share the news. They could read it right across my
face. We went to buy coffee at the small cafeteria near
the main door and all the time Rachel's happy chatter
about her latest shopping bargains and plans for the
weekend mingled with my own inner relief and joy. 'It's
all fine! It's all fine!' The doctor's words went round and
round in my mind, accentuating my delight.

Soon afterwards Les and I walked out into the dull
November morning together and spent a while shopping
in the city before relaxing over a soup and cheesecake
lunch at one of the superstores, 'by way of celebration'!
We drove home in the afternoon twilight, just as the
grey mist had begun to drift eerily in across Loch Skene
to clutch at the nearer woods with its long damp fingers.

Two days later the blood test result came through. It was normal too! This doubling of the good news had an instant beneficial effect and I found myself making all kinds of new plans. Perhaps I could borrow Les's bicycle (Rachel had taken mine to Aberdeen) and try pedalling to the village for our daily supply of bread and vegetables? Then maybe I could start planting out the last daffodil bulbs in the sheltered side border too? And begin a book chapter on prayer, which a publisher had recently suggested? It was amazing how two items of reassuring news could trigger such immediate eagerness and excitement! The necessity for check-ups wasn't nearly so irksome if results proved good; in fact it offered a welcome record of progress.

'You'd better not get too busy!' Les cautioned, frowning at my enthusiasm.

But nothing could crush my relief and gratitude.

'Both test results are normal!' I kept telling myself, pleased the more with each repetition. I was getting well again and gaining new strength. It was now possible (and important) to think in terms of 'health' rather than 'illness', and this switch in emphasis marked a significant step forward. At the same time, thoughts about achieving that sought-after success image began to recede. The need to make a good impression on others didn't seem to matter so much now.

*   *   *

Although Les drew the line at lending his bike for village shopping, I kept to my plan for planting out the daffodil bulbs, and once this was done began work on the prayer chapter, spending several midweek hours at the upstairs desk. The editor had asked for a personal story, and while working on this I became more and more aware of how much prayer had come to mean over recent months.

In gradually growing to love Jesus in a deeper way, times spent with him were no longer a stiff, formal, 'ought-to-do' exercise, but instead offered longed-for companionship. I felt my acute need of him now and, as well as pouring out the bewilderment and sorrow, also tried to tell him of my delight and gratitude. Then, as well, I wanted to be still and listen in order not to hurt him by further insensitivity. I knew I must come to him in quiet prayer for his sake, as well as for my own. And the 'want' and the 'must' had come entirely from Jesus, even as the growing love of our relationship had its only source in him.

As it grew more clear in my thinking, this fact became most wonderful of all. That Jesus should put all within me—first the desire, then the love and devotion for him which would constantly fulfil that desire—seemed so remarkable I could hardly take it in. Until then I had always thought I must work up my own desire for, and trust in Jesus. These were gifts which I, on my own, must first prepare and bring so he could then approve and bless me in some special way.

But it was not like that at all. *Everything* was his! He was responsible for the whole sequence, even from the first moment of faint desire. And so in me, frail, faltering, prone to sin, he somehow gave part of himself back to himself. And he would do so more and more. It was a revolutionary truth, inexplicable yet nonetheless real. And its significance continued to intrigue and stir me as I worked on the chapter, though it was difficult to express this growing inner awareness in words.

As I worked at the bedroom desk I could look out over the river and further woods, and even to the fields beyond, for the trees were now quite leafless. Several water birds had become more visible too, since their protective reed-cover had shrivelled and died. One afternoon I saw a family of mallard ducks foraging near to a flat, downriver rock; a couple of moorhens hopping from one reed island to the next; a dipper pair diving beneath the rushing brown water; and our two resident mute swans preening near a mid-stream island. Then a group of whooper swans flew over, and a single house-martin appeared, swooping desperately back and forth above the grass and river. I was surprised to see it, for the other martins had migrated south more than two months before. Had this one lingered too long? Could it survive much longer?

The sight of all those birds, and the unexpected warmth of the November afternoon, enticed me out into the garden, so I left the prayer chapter half-typed on the desk and set about planting the last crocuses and daffodils in the trough where the pansies had thrived all summer. It gave particular pleasure to press those hard, lifeless-looking bulbs into the cold brown earth 'in certainty of spring', and as I worked (the robin approving from close by) I realized how much stronger I was becoming. This filled me with gratitude and I decided to make a point of sharing the fact with Helen and Anne, our prayer group friends, and the many village neighbours who had stood with us right through our times of anxiety and sorrow. It was important that they should now also enter with us into our growing praise and joy, so over the next few days I told them of my marked improvement whenever we met, and their enthusiastic response added to my own happiness.

I was approaching a more settled phase after all the mental and emotional highs and lows, and this too was reassuring. Prior to the difficult few years we'd just encountered I had always been placid by nature, rarely disturbed, and it had been hard to live with such uncharacteristic mood swings. However, through the experience I had begun to learn not to presume upon a placid personality, nor to look critically at those who struggled with their own repeated ups and downs, for I was just as vulnerable. I knew that now.

*   *   *

Winter came with a first light snowfall, late in November. Murray, concerned as ever for the birds, made a large bowl of pudding from peanuts, dried fruit, oatmeal, and melted lard, and put it out on the birdtable. The response was immediate as blackbirds, chaffinches and tits tried to fight off a horde of greedy starlings and, in the process, knocked the dish upside-down onto the snow below. More than once Murray righted the bowl, and more than once we watched a cluster of tits take advantage of this brief interval between pudding courses by perching on our neighbour's washing line to clean their greasy beaks along a row of just-laundered pillow cases.

It was during the same week of snowy weather that Les bought a well-used motorized lawn mower from a work colleague, 'So the two lads can offer to mow lawns for village neighbours next summer!' he explained, lifting the rusty old thing up onto the kitchen working top. He and Stuart were soon busy checking over various oily engine parts which they scattered everywhere. (How I longed for a garden shed as I watched them.) Then, at last, they fitted everything back together and coaxed the tired old machine into a burst of new life. It was strange to hear the loud throb of a motor-mower on a dark, snowy winter's night.

'But it does give you a foretaste of summer, doesn't it!' Les said afterwards, as he mopped up an oil puddle which had begun to ooze across the formica towards a batch of newly-baked biscuits. 'And that makes all the mess more than worthwhile!'

I had to smile, enjoying Les's pleasure in helping the lads set up a small mowing business for the following summer. They'd need encouragement to get going when the time came, but the thought of extra pocket money to spend on records and a growing collection of tools would soon generate enthusiasm. It was good to be thinking of summer already! But in the meantime Christmas lay just ahead and there were all kinds of exciting preparations to complete. 'Keep everything simple this time, won't you?' Les urged, so I drew up a list of not-too-demanding festive plans and, for most of our presents, used items bought earlier in the year from a gift catalogue.

These different ideas and preparations gave special pleasure and the more I thought of our approaching celebration, the more I determined it would be a time of quiet, simple appreciation, rather than busy, elaborate festivity. There was so much for which to praise God this year. Despite all, he had enriched our lives in countless different ways since our last Christmas together.

Amid the gladness of such planning I found it very difficult to accept a sudden, unexpected return of extreme weakness and nausea. There was so much I wanted to do and yet the only way to cope with the problem was to lie down and relax. Some strength returned after a few hours of rest, and then I was able to get up and start on one or two small tasks again. But it was hard to be content with such restrictions. I longed to make some constructive use of those rest times, so decided to spend them in quiet thought and prayer, remembering different friends, such as Isobel in her loneliness, and Irene recovering from her serious operation. Was she, too, going through this experience of recurrent weariness? In her case it would be far more taxing and prolonged, particularly if debilitating after-treatment had been needed. It was reassuring to be able to pray for Isobel and Irene, also for some of our village friends facing hard circumstances. As I did so I wished I could help in practical ways but, since that was not possible for the time being, prayer became all the more valuable. I could pray with increased awareness of their difficulties now, and in this way was taken out beyond myself and my weakness. Such an opportunity became very important to me during those long December days. Perhaps more important than ever before.

There was additional time for reading too, and a book by Professor Blaiklock* helped me further to understand the purpose of suffering. He wrote of a cross as 'being at the centre of our faith and we dare not ask to fly from this'. Why mustn't we seek an escape? I questioned, then remembered that if Jesus accepted suffering so too must we. Furthermore, Jesus became one with us through suffering to a degree we might not otherwise experience. The significance of this became the more real to me as I lay and quietly considered it further, for it confirmed that all of Jesus' resources to cope with suffering could be ours too. As Professor Blaiklock put it, 'salvation means quiet of heart and mind amid conflict'. The 'amid'

* E. M. Blaiklock *Still a Christian* (Hodder & Stoughton). By permission.

comforted me. Jesus understood my frustration at being laid low just when I was doing so well. He knew how eager I was to get back on top so I could reach immediate goals. But meanwhile he was again teaching me to lean back and rest so I could draw on his offered gift of stillness in place of my natural disappointment.

I thought back to the happy optimism of just a few days earlier. Cheerfulness had been in easy supply then. Now it had to be squeezed out. Perhaps Jesus was wanting me also to recognize that my own resources of cheerfulness and courage were limited and so soon exhausted.

I was discovering again that I must find all I needed in Jesus. In fact it had now become not so much a looking for new resources from him as an intense longing to possess more and more of Jesus himself, and to be possessed the more by him. How could such a mutual possession be? I thought and thought about this, trying to grasp the wonder of Jesus desiring to possess us, and at the same time offering himself for our possession. The 'how' of this was beyond my limited human understanding. I only knew that the relationship which had begun when, as a teenager, I had first given myself to him must, if it was to prove effective, go on growing and deepening. In this way it would become constantly more strong and full of joy until one day, beyond death, I would become entirely his, and he more fully mine.

How valuable those times of rest and quiet gradually became as, through the Holy Spirit, I was moved to love and worship Jesus with a fervour I had never known before. There was still the irksomeness of feeling weak and unwell, but this very sense of need laid me further open to Jesus' tenderness, putting me in a place where he comforted me the more. I was amazed and very much humbled by this.

And then, as December continued, strength slowly returned and I was able to care for the family once again. Les kept a close eye on my activities, though, insisting that I stay in bed until after breakfast each morning. The fact that he worked shift hours meant he was able to take over the household tasks when necessary (what an asset this had been through the previous months too), and I appreciated Les's thoughtfulness, though was anxious lest I should take advantage of him.

'I'm only going to let you run the show for a day or two,' I'd keep reminding him. 'And then it will be my turn again!'

Actually, when Les brought me breakfast in bed or insisted on doing the washing and ironing, I found it quite pleasant to be fussed over again, though I didn't want to cling to such fussing now. The gradual overall progress into health had come to mean much more than any questionable advantage to be gained from trying to prolong the illness.

At the same time I now knew how easy it would be for people to become hypochondriacs. A lengthy illness could become an acceptable way of life, influencing people's outlooks to such an extent that they would not want to be told, 'Now you're on the mend!' lest this disturb their new-found security. In fact any such suggestion about a return to health would be likely to trigger renewed symptoms of illness introduced (perhaps unconsciously) as a protective device, even though they might seem outwardly pleased to be informed of progress.

I recognized now that such people had deep and genuine problems, particularly with insecurity. Someone needed to spend time with them, offering constructive sympathy and exploring their insistence on prolonging an illness when they could be free from its limitations. What was the root cause of their hypochondria? How could it be overcome? I couldn't help remembering how I had despised hypochondriac patients during nursing training, feeling reluctant to give them the attention I considered others more readily deserved. But would I brush them aside now? Or would I try, if they felt able to respond, to reach through to the hurting part inside which so desperately craved ongoing concern from others? Specialist skills would probably be required before such people could be set completely free, but nonetheless I needed to react differently towards such people in future, feeling with them and trying to understand, while still not overlooking their need for a radical change in attitude.

I knew, too, that it was important to differentiate between hypochondriacs and people working through a difficult adjustment. I was still at that stage. Such people, frightened by an encounter with serious illness, suddenly became hypersensitive, afraid lest the least lump or bump should have sinister implications. And so, anxious about ailments, and worried by the various aches and pains associated with normal healing from surgery, they frequented the doctor's consulting room, longing for reassurance yet at the same time being strangely hesitant to accept it, even when repeatedly offered.

The medical profession probably found it hard often to be confronted by such a person and yet, exacting though it was, the patient needed constant gentleness and understanding, someone to listen while newly accumulated fear was released once again. In time it would stop accumulating as a doctor's reassurance was gradually believed and accepted, but all of this—the repeated visits to the surgery and the verbal releasing of fear—far from being hypochondria, was part of a long coming-to-terms-with-it sequence which refused to be hurried along.

I had come to understand, as the weeks and months passed, that I could not be relieved of my concerns once and for all, in one moment of time. It was a lengthy mental and emotional progression, hard to explain and no doubt puzzling to friends who showed such understanding for the straightforward physical side of my problem. But nevertheless it *was* a progression. I would get there! I would, at last, reach a place of settled calm, but meanwhile I very much needed medical people to stand patiently alongside and encourage, listen, feel, and hope with me. How very much I appreciated all who did.

10

The Inescapable Mosaic

One day, when I was feeling stronger, a long-standing friend, Susan, drove up from Perth to have lunch with us. A tedious journey for much of the way, yet she came gladly out of genuine concern. This gift of herself and her time made a considerable impression upon me, and we had the happiest of days together sitting by the fireside and catching up on family news. Susan's coming greatly refreshed me!

Next day, aware of the approaching deadline on the prayer chapter, I decided to spend several hours typing the final draft in readiness for the post the following morning. After an hour or so at the upstairs desk, the whole project began to come together and the pleasure of writing gradually took over from the hard grind of sitting down and forcing thoughts out onto paper. I began to feel relieved and excited, almost exhilarated. The chapter was developing into a presentable form at last. It would soon be complete!

Then the doorbell rang. 'Probably just the postman with a parcel,' I thought, going slowly downstairs, my mind still assembling the next sentence. It was the Murdoch family, passing our way and wondering, 'If we could call in for a while?' I smiled and showed them into the livingroom, all the time thinking, 'Will there be time to finish the chapter? Will I be able to recapture that elusive flow?'

It was hard to be welcoming. Pleasure at the Murdoch's

unexpected arrival had to be forced out and no doubt sounded false. But then I thought, 'What about all those recent resolves to devote more time to people? Is it more important to sit and write today, or to give myself to these friends, appreciating their thoughtfulness in deciding to spend a few hours with me?' I struggled with the question for several more minutes, all the time trying to keep up an easy-going conversation with Jean and Simon while the three boys played around our feet. Should I offer them coffee? Some lunch too? Or perhaps they needed to be on their way? At last I brought myself round to considering, 'What is the *right* thing to do in this situation?' and knew straightaway that it was to give myself completely to the family for as long as they wanted to stay by our fireside. Once that basic question had been settled I was slowly able to relax, appreciating the warmth of their friendship just as I had appreciated Susan's the day before.

The family stayed for coffee, then a snack lunch, leaving around 2 p.m. Later I completed a few more paragraphs of the chapter without too much difficulty, and estimated it would be ready for the post a couple of days later, still well within the deadline. That evening, looking back over the day, I knew I could now feel glad the Murdochs had come. Through their visit I had been given an opportunity to learn, in practice rather than mere theory, the rightness of offering full, unhurried attention to others. And in the process had quite unexpectedly discovered an even greater pleasure in their friendship, something I would have missed had the day's plan not been interrupted. It was important that friends should continue to call 'in passing', for in this way my learning could progress and our friendships be further strengthened.

Once the chapter had been posted off, I busied myself with the remaining Christmas preparations on my list. Murray helped stir the cake and pudding during a half-day off from school and by the time Les and Stuart arrived home that evening the whole of our open-plan living area was filled with a delicious spicy aroma.

'Wow, that smells fantastic, Mum!' Stuart exclaimed, eyes shining. 'Did Murray leave me the bowl to lick?' Then, after supper, a strange, unwelcome smell began to replace the spiciness. Les and Stuart were determined to doctor some more of the mower's oily innards and before long had rigged up some kind of diagnostic experiment in order to discover a cause for its most recent problems. I glanced across the room and saw the pair of them poring over a glass tumbler of water into which they'd placed the mower's fuel chamber and a teaspoon.

'Whatever next in here!' I protested.

Les glanced round. 'Don't tell me you're about to turn our workshop into a kitchen!' he objected, putting on his mock-innocence expression.

I sighed, then smiled a little. That same day our next-door neighbour had been creosoting his brand new garden shed, and storing tools and machinery inside. I'd watched with envy.

'Well, how about a garden shed for Christmas?' I suggested.

'Now, *that's* an idea!' Les responded, laughing to himself. Maybe for the year after next?'

A first blizzard blew up that night, flinging itself against the side of the house so fiercely that the wooden wall boards and roof joists creaked in loud protest. By morning the storm had spent itself, leaving the world around us to rest for a while beneath a thick cover of glistening snow. Such a transformation! I opened the bedroom window, pushing it out against a window-ledge snowdrift, and stood looking across the river, feeling the stinging cold against my face. The water was steel-grey and thick with moving ice islands which jostled each other around each snow-capped boulder. There were no birds in sight except for the mute swan pair dabbling unperturbed, their feathers grubby-looking against the intensely white snow.

Flocks of blackbirds, tits and starlings arrived from the woods, desperate for another of Murray's oatmeal puddings, and on the way out to them with a bowlful my head brushed against the rotary washing line, setting its numerous rows of ice beads tinkling like glass. The pudding dish would hardly fit onto the bird table for its protective roof was now thickly thatched in white and the floor had been carpeted to match, but the starlings pushed in to gobble at their breakfast, leaving all the other birds to squabble over crusts of bread scattered across our neighbour's lawn.

A couple of days later I helped with a Christmas tea at the church hall to which friends from a psychiatric hospital had been invited, and it was rewarding to see the sudden excitement on those often-sad faces when one of the tea ladies arrived after the meal, carefully disguised as Santa, and carrying a black plastic bag full of gifts.

The twilight lingered on that afternoon, and when Les drove up to collect me we stood in the hall car park for a few moments enjoying the wide, white view which stretched far out across the valley and beyond. Distant Bennachie was only snow-dusted but nearer fields and rooftops were a dazzling white, and thick snow was spread out in fingers along the branch tips of close-by fir trees, as if each was wearing several pairs of kid gloves. Soon after reaching the house we were treated to an impressive fly past of whooper swans. I heard their approaching calls, loud and laboured, and rushed to the window, just glimpsing the flock of five as they glowed faint gold in the light cast by the street lamps. What a sight! What beauty everywhere around us on a bitterly cold midwinter's day!

We mustn't ever get used to it all!' I told Les. 'Because that would be to miss out on so much joy.'

More snow fell. Perhaps we would have a white Christmas? Excitement mounted as the village schools broke up in a flurry of parties and festive 'fayres'. Soon the street around us was alive with eager voices as muffled-up children set off for the nearby hill slope, pulling assorted toboggans, some made of wooden slats, some of light-weight metal, but most of plastic in bright red, yellow or blue. Mothers passed our front door, dragging toddlers along on newly-bought sledges, returning later with the day's shopping piled in alongside

the small rosy-cheeked passenger. Snowdays were fun
for everyone. All except for Miss Puss. She loathed such
a cold and unnecessary intrusion and had to be forced to
go outside two or three times a day, becoming all the
more angry if the quick door-slam which followed dis-
lodged an avalanche of snow from the wide overhanging
eaves. More than once we had to hurry out and rescue
her from sudden burial.

Christmas was almost with us! I fetched three favourite
records of carols down from an upstairs cupboard and
played them over and over again, letting their message
of certainty and joy penetrate deep into my heart and
mind. The meaning of Christmas had suddenly become
extra vivid, more to be treasured than ever before. I
could not forget the poignancy of Jesus' coming to us in
such a way, and all so that we might be brought out of
darkness into light, out of sorrow into joy, out of death
into the most complete life of all. How could such a
magnificent truth ever be grasped or fully understood?

*   *   *

A few days before Christmas I picked up a newspaper
and read that David Watson was seriously ill again, his
condition deteriorating. The liver growth had started to
enlarge, despite the urgent prayers and strong faith of
thousands of people across the world. A great sadness
welled up inside me as I read the short paragraph two or
three times, slowly taking the news in. All along, Les and
I had continued to pray for David, following his progress
with more-than-usual interest, and drawing much personal encouragement from it. But now he was rapidly
weakening. The doctors could do no more.

My mind centred on David and his family for the rest
of the day. I could not forget them, for in a hard to
explain way I now found myself linked in a close, unexpected bond with others suffering from cancer, even
though most faced circumstances far worse than my
own. Their joy had become mine and their eager hope
offered me strength during darker times. But what

about when a setback occurred? What then?

Sadness and apprehension were already pushing back against my mind. I felt it for David and his wife and, through them, for myself. Such empathy was part of this close interweaving. Until now I had not realized that hardship could so bind our different lives together, making them one. A oneness of strength, but inevitably of sorrow too, and in both our need for each other was very great. The weaving was valuable. I wanted and needed it, despite the pain. But how could I help? What could I do for David now?

I went up to the bedroom and in the early evening darkness prayed for David and his family, asking God still to be a strong refuge to them, a sheltering place where fear and overwhelming disappointment could not intrude. A place most of all, of stillness and peace and acceptance. I did not know how else to pray, for there was no inner conviction concerning healing, only an awareness of what I was just beginning to understand. The inexplicable calm—even solemn joy—of relinquishment to a God who was still in complete command of the situation, still able even to enrich because of it.

Tears came as I prayed. They were mostly for David and his wife Anne, and for the whole heavy sorrow of suffering. Perhaps too for what I, in small part, had come to know of it. Not tears of anger nor, anymore, of inward fear, but simply of overwhelming sadness which could be relieved in no other way.

And slowly, unexpectedly, I began to understand that such a sorrow was as much a part of Christmas as all the joy. The joy of Jesus' birth had been woven in with the sorrow of Mary's pain, and the joy of the wise men's rich gifts with the terror of Herod's plot. Then too, so much later on, the tremendous joy of our deliverance from wrongdoing and eternal punishment had only come at the agonizing cost of Jesus' crucifixion. And I realized it must always be, such was the inescapable mosaic of our present life.

Yet the pattern would not continue indefinitely. One day it would be dramatically interrupted when Jesus led

us on into a whole new context of life, full of unshadowed
glory. Was David soon to go on into that immense joy,
even though so many still prayed and believed for his
healing? Yet surely such an interruption would not be
defeat but healing and homecoming and high honour
all at one time, despite the keen sorrow of loss?

I tried to think of it in such a way, but the sorrow was
still there. The heavy sadness. Sometimes it was very
hard still to hold firmly to the certainty of joy.

Did Les sense my sadness when I went back downstairs?
Perhaps it was obvious from my face. He reached out a
hand and drew me down to sit beside him on the settee.

'Come and help me open all these Christmas cards!'
So we enjoyed the day's mail together (I hadn't had time
to do so earlier) and amongst the cards was a short,
loving message from friends in America who had just
heard of my illness: 'We're praying much for you'. Beneath their words were these lines:

> *I know that nothing is mightier than God—*
> *not the severest hardship, nor the deepest distress.*
> *His power to help is always greater.*

What a statement! I read it several times, trying to mem-
orize each line so the words would become mine. They
were strong and secure, a clearcut affirmation which
again emphasized how every adversity—even the worst
of all—could never be outside the power or scope of
God. As God he would always be mightier still, and
therefore completely able to help. Through those words
Jesus strengthened my trust once more and lifted me up
so that, even if only briefly, I felt higher still than all the
sorrow, able to glimpse the unshadowed glory where all
sorrow would one day be over, all pain left far behind.

What tender comfort Jesus gave that evening when my
sadness was so great. How deeply I loved him for it, and
how I longed somehow to convey my love to him. But he
knew. This love had been of his giving too, put within
me so I might know the delight of such an inclusion.

I I

Nothing Can Win against God!

Christmas Eve came and around mid-morning the post-man delivered a last large bundle of cards. Hidden among them was a long white self-addressed envelope, very thin. It was a reply from the editor of the book for which I had written the chapter on prayer. He had accepted my manuscript. What a relief! Now I could really relax and enjoy our celebrations.

Rachel had already joined us for her two-week holi-day, so that morning she and Murray made mince pies and iced the Christmas cake while Les and I drove off to deliver a few small gifts in the village. I saved our visit to Miss Emily until last, wanting to give her as much time as possible. There was no slow approach of footsteps after our knock on the door, only a faint call. 'Come awa' in!'

We found Miss Emily in bed, very low and discouraged. The bright, eager gleam had gone from her pale blue eyes and I felt immediately concerned. 'I'm just awfu' tired and sair,' she explained in a whisper, then turned her face slowly toward me and smiled a little. I sat down at the bedside and took her small, very thin hand.

'Then maybe it's best for you to stay here and rest today.'

'Aye, but I'll hope to be up the morn.' She sighed and lay back further against the pillow.

'Did you know it's Christmas Eve?' I asked after a while.

Miss Emily opened her eyes wide and gazed at me.

'Is't?' She allowed the information to register, then said, 'Och, but I'm nae thinking o' the days noo . . .'

Les had been standing in the dark doorway of the room holding our gift and, feeling spare, went to put it on the old sideboard in the adjoining room. Miss Emily saw the shadowy movement.

'Who's there?' she demanded, startled.

'Just Les. He's leaving a small present ready in the next room for you.'

Miss Emily relaxed and reached out her other hand towards me.

'I would be a lost person if I didnae hae God,' she said suddenly, running her fingers slowly down the soft sleeve of my coat. 'Aye, I'd be a lost person . . .'

We sat in silence for a few minutes, drawing comfort from the pleasure of being together. Miss Emily seemed to brighten a little and when Les came quietly back to the doorway she said, 'And today I can be happy because ye've baith come to see me!'

We talked on until the clock on the sideboard struck twelve.

'I'll have to go, it's lunchtime!' I told Miss Emily. 'But we'll visit you again soon!'

How hard it was to leave her alone in her room. But then, while hesitating in the doorway, I remembered a close neighbour would soon be bringing Miss Emily's lunch, and others were planning to visit her later in the day. She would not be on her own for very long.

'Cheerio!' Miss Emily called to us, her voice low and hoarse. 'Cheerio! Cheerio!'

It was her usual way of saying farewell. Several 'cheerios' one after the other, accompanied by as many waves and smiles. But this time Miss Emily was too tired to wave. She only smiled. A slow smile which briefly lit up her blue eyes, reminding me of all the past times when we had laughed and talked together, and her eyes had shone.

By now the day was cold and damp, 'dreich' as Miss Emily would have said, and the last of the snow had all but dripped away. After lunch I went out along the river bank in the sleety rain and collected broom sprigs and pods, some grasses, the last of the scarlet rosehips, and a cow-parsley seedhead. The foaming river, high and brown after the thaw, was rushing right over the largest boulders and, just above the beeches, a crow was drifting fast with the wind, wingtips ragged against the grey clouds.

It was a relief to return to the warm kitchen and, once indoors, I laid my winter's posy in a circle on the dining table, adding a red candle and ribbons of matching crepe paper to make a centrepiece for our Christmas Eve tea. The broadcast carol service from Cambridge had begun so, when the arrangement was complete, I lay down on the settee and listened. It was such a majestic portrayal of Jesus' long-planned coming into a suffering world.

While I listened, Rachel and the boys decorated the livingroom with colourful paper streamers and stars, then Rachel brought her home-grown orange tree down from upstairs and set it beside the main window before hanging each thin branch with scarlet balls and strands of silver foil. Last of all she arranged our African nativity scene around the base of the tree. I watched her at work, seeing how the pale green citrus leaves made a perfect canopy for the circle of carved wooden figures below.

'It's a different kind of Christmas tree this year!' Rachel explained, coming across to sit beside me. And for a few moments we paused together, appreciating its simple beauty.

Murray was busy fitting a tall white candle into the wrought iron holder kept for Christmas-time.

'Is that going to be our Peace Candle?' I asked and, silent as ever, he nodded, before setting it in the main window for passers-by to see. Stuart had spent the best part of an hour bustling round in his usual exuberant fashion, hanging row upon row of Christmas cards along the pinewood beams, then, 'How about celebrating with lots and lots more candles?' he cried. 'Haven't you got a whole boxful somewhere, Mum?'

He rummaged around in the kitchen drawers, found

the supply of white emergency candles, and set them in improvised holders all over the living area so there wouldn't be a single unlit corner.

'That's about it now!' he announced. 'The room's ready for Christmas, so when's it going to be time for our special tea?'

It was very dark outside so we drew the curtains against the cold wet night, leaving an opening where the Peace Candle stood. Rachel heated up her mince pies and sausage rolls, Les laid the table, the lads helped set out bowls of nuts and fruit, and I made a frill for the cake before putting it beside the table centrepiece. We were ready!

'Let's eat by candlelight!' Stuart decided as soon as we'd all sat down, so Murray leapt up and mischievously plunged the room into darkness while Stuart fumbled for the matches.

One by one he lit the white candles around the room, then Murray's slender Peace Candle in the window, and last of all the centrepiece candle set amid the rough interweaving of riverside twigs. Soon the room was full of flickering flames and dancing shadows as the golden light reached out to its furthest corners and touched the small orange tree sheltering the manger scene with its gentle radiance. For a few moments I sat in silence, hardly hearing the family's excited chatter as they tucked in to our celebration meal.

'Even a single candle flame is stronger than a whole room full of darkness!' I realized, gazing round at such pure, exquisite beauty. Words from one of the Cambridge carol service readings came to my mind: 'The light shines in the darkness, and the darkness has not overcome it' (Jn 1:5).

What a vivid truth! In that moment of recognition it was as if a single candle had been lit deep within my own mind, further illuminating that powerful earlier statement . . . I know that nothing is mightier than God.

It was true. Nothing could win against God. Nothing at all. The light would always be greater than even the deepest darkness. What reassurance! What joy! What

magnificent cause for celebration! And on this Christmas
Eve more than on any I had known before.

*   *   *

Les and I enjoyed a peaceful, gradual awakening next
morning, the rest of the family still being fast asleep at
8.45 a.m., in marked contrast to Christmas mornings of
only a few years before. I was glad our minister had
planned to celebrate the occasion with Communion, and
the service was full of the same mingled solemnity and
praise. We walked home afterwards in the clear pale-
gold sunlight and, after lunch and gift-giving, Les drove
us to Aberdeen for tea and games with Win and Priscilla
and the family. Their thoughtfulness in this way completed the pleasure of our Christmas and much later, as
the day ended, we came home through the dark empty
countryside, taking the lochside route where tall, leafless
trees were all silver with moonlight.

'It's been an extra happy Christmas!' I whispered to
Les as we rounded the last corner and saw all the village
lights ahead.

He nodded. 'Yes, the Lord has been very good to us.
And not just today either!'

Les's day shift week began very early next morning
and the rest of us were still in bed when he left home,
but I woke in time to see the thick dark boles of the
beech trees turn gold in the first glow of dawn. After a
quick breakfast I set off for a walk, eager to be out in the
sunlit stillness and, just beyond the back step, found the
first daffodil shoots pushing bravely up in the plastic
trough. The Don was still running high above the boulders, robbing the dippers of their much-prized midstream
perches, but I noticed a few blackheaded gulls travelling
happily downriver with the swift current, repeatedly
bill-dipping en route.

Beyond the wide bend moles had cast up several
mounds of rich brown earth, now hardened and dusted
with white, and in a sheltered hollow a carpet of frost-
stiffened leaves had been transformed into a delicate

tracery of shapes and vein-patterns. I stood and looked
at their simple loveliness, then at the wild rose bushes
close by, thin branches sheathed in glistening hoar frost,
then at the dark tumble of the river. Everything around
me expressed God's great goodness, everything reflected
his grandeur. If only I could tell him how much such
magnificence meant! And how the firm order and pur-
posefulness of his creation now so often consoled and
reassured me! But I couldn't find a way to say it. None
of the words I tried out in my mind sounded right. So I
stood in silence in the cold, piercing sunlight for a little
longer, and then turned back towards the house. The
youngsters would be up by now, I guessed, and no
doubt eating their way through huge helpings of corn-
flakes and toast. I needed to get myself organized for
the day, and make up the spare bed too. A family friend,
Patrick, was due to arrive for an overnight visit some
time during the week.

He came just before the New Year, eager to discuss
ideas for a missionary magazine with which he was involved. While we talked on that cold December day our
conversation began to move out in other directions too,
as we shared reactions to different experiences in our
lives. Before I could stop myself I had begun to put
some of the accumulated thoughts of recent weeks into
words, grateful for this unexpected opportunity to try to
express them all, even if falteringly.

Patrick understood what I was speaking about. He
knew what it was like to go on and on grappling with
recurrent mental, emotional and physical difficulties until, at last, you begin to lay hold of some sort of purpose
and meaning. He knew how hard it was to live all at once
with joy and sorrow, hope and fear, laughter and tears.
He was able to come alongside in a way few others could
do, intuitively aware of my still-present need to talk
things out. How often over those long winter weeks I
had longed to release still-accumulating questions and
reactions, but I had repeatedly held back, not wanting to
take another person's time, and uncertain, too, as to
whether they could understand so long and complex a

bewilderment.

Patrick sipped the mid-morning coffee I had made. Then he turned and said, 'Would you feel able to tell me the whole story, right from the start until now? Would it help you to do so?'

I valued his perception and willingness to listen, though was careful to keep the sharing as brief as possible, not wanting to labour my difficulties. The relief of opening up to a person who was totally outside my personal situation, yet nonetheless full of fellow-feeling, was immediate.

This time (now more than six months after the operation) I needed to find words for a continuing uneasiness triggered by the news of David Watson's hard struggle with liver secondaries. There was no reason to be afraid for, in contrast, I had been given an excellent prognosis, but I remained strangely vulnerable and in need of people to be patient and understanding with me for just a little longer.

Patrick knew this. He didn't leap back into our conversation with a quick unconvincing, 'Don't worry, I'm sure everything will be all right!' Instead he sat in silence after I had finished speaking, allowing a time of reflective quiet before he began slowly, 'Elaine, always remember that everything which happens in our lives, everything, has come by God's allowing. And for this reason he can keep us completely safe through it all. What's more, everything he allows, whether it brings happiness or sadness, is part of his good pattern for us.'

Patrick paused, and I could tell his mind was reaching back over his own life. 'God wants to bless you—he's already blessing you!—in ways you couldn't otherwise have known. Discipline your mind to dwell constantly on this truth, then fear will be robbed of its influence. It won't be able to rush in and swamp you any more because you'll have a stronger answer.'

It couldn't have been easy for Patrick to reach so positive a conclusion after the considerable personal distress and sorrow I knew he had experienced. Yet this one certainty had now come to override all else, and his conviction made a strong impression upon me.

Furthermore, I could see now that the certainty of 'every circumstance being designed for our enrichment' had to be based upon first knowing Jesus in the unique, transforming oneness which I was beginning to experience through adversity. The more real Jesus became to me, the more convinced I was of his utter goodness, and as a result could accept that everything he allowed *was* designed for my enrichment. Surely this was one of the principal ways in which his love for me would be expressed! At the same time this certainty was becoming the eventual answer for my bewilderment and apprehension. I no longer needed to demand answers and explanations as a prerequisite to offering him my trust. If Jesus' prime intention was that I should be enriched, so emphasizing his goodness the more, then that was enough. I could believe, full stop. So I was completely safe and secure.

It was a still more detailed development of the many new things Jesus had been showing me over the months. Another vital, real-life lesson, made the more convincing by Patrick's clear presentation. How wise Jesus was to show me each stage at the right time, in the right context, and only when I became ready. And I realized that, as the long year ended and we went on into all the varied circumstances ahead, Jesus had given me a whole additional dimension of truth to welcome and delight in. A dimension I would have hardly recognized, let alone welcomed, just a year before.

At that time I had considered I knew and possessed so much, now I had been emptied out. But as a direct result Jesus had begun to fill the emptiness, offering in himself all I could ever desire, all I could ever need. And he had come to me not in spite of suffering, but because of it. The suffering had been, for me, essential. I could not understand why this was so. I only knew now, with wonder, that it was true.

*   *   *

Patrick left next morning and then, two days later, it was New Year's Eve, a much celebrated occasion in our village. That night a gale blew up and the angry wind came roaring through the beech woods, determined finally to drag down the twigs and small branches it had menaced during earlier onslaughts.

Rachel and the lads planned to welcome in the New Year at a friend's house nearby, so had baths and tidied themselves up before setting off into the storm. Rachel and Murray left first, full of laughing excitement. Stuart followed, sullen and silent, slamming the door behind him. He was angry because Murray had mischievously tried to float one of his shoes in the bath and now it was oozing water at every step!

Les and I breathed a simultaneous sigh of relief when the house fell silent at last and, pulling the settee close to the electric fire, talked for a while, thinking back over the year.

'How about reading a psalm before we go to bed?' Les suggested. 'Let's choose one that's specially appropriate for New Year's Eve.' He took his favourite Revised Standard Version from the bookshelf and chose Psalm 139, reading it slowly through.

> Thou dost beset me behind and before,
> and layest thy hand upon me.

The force of those statements, so often appropriate in the past during the many different circumstances we'd faced together, now held even greater meaning. At no point during the past year had God ignored or forgotten us. He had been there, whether or not we had thought of him and reached out to take his offered help. More remarkable still, he had not given up on us, despite all the doubts and depression. And his hand was still laid upon us in preparation for the year ahead.

We knelt down together and praised and prayed, full of gratitude for remembered blessings—Les's work, the meeting of every practical need, our home and beautiful surroundings, the many friends and family members

who had cared so thoughtfully for us, returning health
and a more settled peace . . .

Then, still there by the fireside, we gave ourselves, our
children, and the whole unknown year to God, full of
new gladness as we did so. So many hard, dark times
were over, never to be experienced, never even to be
remembered again. We were already walking on into
the light of growing understanding, a light no darkness
could overcome.

> . . .even the darkness is not dark to thee,
> the night is bright as the day   (Ps 139:12).

Conclusion

More than a year has passed since that stormy December night and now, looking back, the events of intervening months seem to be mostly a mingling of ordinary things. Nonetheless, one or two memories stand out, distinct because of their particular significance.

The first is sad. One Sunday, a few weeks after the New Year began, we heard that David Watson had died. Someone told Les at church, and he shared the news with us over lunch. In the brief silence which followed I tried to grasp that David was actually with Jesus now, seeing and delighting in him 'face to face'. The long suffering was finally over.

Two or three weeks later we listened to recordings of the last sermons David had preached and I couldn't help noticing his emphasis on taking refuge in God, 'dwelling in the shelter of the Most High,' as he put it, using the opening words of Psalm 91. For David the safety and calm of such a sheltering place was now complete, eternal. I tried to keep this thought uppermost as I listened to his tired, failing voice, feeling again the poignancy of those last few weeks.

The day before David died the small book on death, *Beyond the Winter Night** was published. It was a Friday, much the same as any other, and as I had received advance copies of the book a few weeks earlier, I forgot the date's significance until a local radio station tele-

* Elaine Brown, *Beyond the Winter Night* (Kingsway Publications 1984).

phoned, requesting a short interview. One or two other small contacts with the media followed, and over the next few months a trickle of letters arrived, as well as invitations to speak at meetings, most of them in our north-eastern area. On these occasions I found people wanted to sit and discuss their own struggles with bereavement or serious illness, needing someone to feel with them and know the anguish without first having to be given lengthy, painful explanations. And, as the weeks went by, I found I could and must understand. I knew now, at least in some measure. The book helped others because those who shared their experiences in its pages had spoken with openness and honesty out of concern for other sufferers. I had a responsibility to follow the example they'd set, and to be glad to give myself if, by so doing, another person's sorrow could be a little eased.

*   *   *

And now a whole new pathway of caring and sharing has opened out to me! Sometimes, though, it is hard to have the needed strength for such a giving, for it inevitably makes demands upon physical and mental resources. So after these times spent with others I try to withdraw for a day or two of rest and refreshment, and in this way a measure of energy is soon restored.

Apart from occasional bouts of fatigue and nausea I am making steady progress. Test results continue to be normal. I can enjoy cycle trips to the village once more (when Les bought me a bicycle for my birthday I was as thrilled as a child would have been), and for most of the time I forget the whole illness experience. Only when some small incident provokes a rush of incredulous remembrance do I think, 'Did it all really happen to me?' And then the inescapable truth thrusts back like a stab of pain. But it is soon past.

Not so with the effect of 'negativism'. I am still very susceptible to this. After exposure to a 'gloom and doom' atmosphere and its accompanying discouragement, I find it difficult to cope for a while. Fear returns, lurking at the threshold of my mind. So much everyday conversation tends to remain focused on problems, illnesses, disappointments and apprehension, unless a disciplined effort is made to turn and look at circumstances from a more constructive angle.

Only then, when openness to a positive approach has brought new hope, can any meaning, solution or healing be found for these heavy, seemingly insoluble ills. I know I've become hypersensitive to negativism now, but that is only because I find its effect so crushing, and particularly at times when my own frail faith is in need— more than all else—of careful nurture.

Perhaps I will remain vulnerable for a long time yet, readily influenced by outward circumstances and inner reactions. The whole long experience continues to have its far-reaching effects.

But now, as I complete this writing on a sunlit early May morning (the riverside sycamores are decked with pale green leaf buds, and wild daffodils, much-frilled and vivid gold, are crowding the far woods) I find myself reaching ahead into the future with a growing inner certainty.

Before long I *will* be fully well again. Then I will think only of the value of my adversity, for all the frustration will have been finally left behind.

So there will be yet more joy! A solemn joy—and greater still for its solemnity.

The Risk

by Jenny Cooke

Jenny was alone. As a child, friends were distant. Later romance was stormy, and love brought pain.

And there was God. Somewhere God. He seemed harder to befriend than anyone. But he was leading her. Even that darkness in her mind—was that guidance?... That broken engagement... the identity crisis of motherhood... the frustrations and the joys of teaching the deaf... her husband's redundancy and search for work... and, through it all, the intense longing to write. It had all been leading to life's highest calling.

To be fully human. To be a Christian. Whether in cosmic leaps or steps of simple trust, she knew it was the wildest, sanest risk that she could ever take.

JENNY COOKE'S writing gift was displayed in her first best-seller *The Cross Behind Bars*. Now in this moving and powerful account of her own spiritual pilgrimage, we see Jenny representing modern man in his search for meaning and love.

Kingsway Publications

David

by Marie Rothenberg and Mel White

On March 3rd, 1983 a despondent father set fire to the room where his six-year-old son lay sleeping. Young David received third-degree burns over ninety percent of his body. Somehow he survived.

This is his mother Marie's story. With compelling honesty she relates her struggle to forgive, and her desperate battle to nurse David back to health. Here we also see a young couple radiate the warmth of Christian fellowship, supporting Marie in her hours of hopelessness and doubt, to a point where the dawn of a new future could overcome the black shadows of the past.

David is a book that looks tragedy in the face and, with no quick and easy solutions, affirms the supremacy of love and life over guilt and despair.

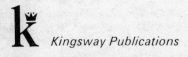

Kingsway Publications